Stoeger Publishing
Great Outdoor Books Since 1925

STOEGER PUBLISHING COMPANY IS A DIVISION OF BENELLI U.S.A.

BENELLI U.S.A.
Vice President and General Manager:
  Stephen Otway
Director of Brand Marketing and
Communications:
  Stephen McKelvain
Vice President of Sales/Strategic Marketing:
  Jack Muety

STOEGER PUBLISHING COMPANY
President: Jeffrey Reh
Publisher: Jay Langston
Managing Editor: Harris J. Andrews
Design & Production Director:
  Cynthia T. Richardson
Photography Director: Alex Bowers
Imaging Specialist: William Graves
Editorial Assistant: Christine Lawton
Design & Production: Susan K. White
Proofreader: Celia Beattie

Published by Stoeger Publishing Company
17603 Indian Head Highway, Suite 200
Accokeek, Maryland 20607

BK0309
ISBN: 0-88317-253-4

Library of Congress Control Number:
2002110070

Manufactured in the United States of America.

Distributed to the book trade and
to the sporting goods trade by:
Stoeger Industries
17603 Indian Head Highway, Suite 200
Accokeek, Maryland 20607
301-283-6300 Fax: 301-283-6986
www.stoegerindustries.com

OTHER PUBLICATIONS:
Shooter's Bible 2004 - 95th Edition
  The World's Standard Firearms
  Reference Book
Gun Trader's Guide - 26th Edition
  Complete Fully Illustrated
  Guide to Modern Firearms with
  Current Market Values

HUNTING & SHOOTING
Hounds of the World
The Turkey Hunter's Tool Kit:
  Shooting Savvy
Hunt Club Management Guide
Archer's Bible
The Truth About
  Spring Turkey Hunting
  According to "Cuz"
The Whole Truth About
  Spring Turkey Hunting
  According to "Cuz"
Complete Book of Whitetail Hunting
Hunting and Shooting
  with the Modern Bow
The Ultimate in Rifle Accuracy
Advanced Black Powder Hunting
Labrador Retrievers
Hunting America's Wild Turkey
Taxidermy Guide
Cowboy Action Shooting
Great Shooters of the World

COLLECTING BOOKS
Sporting Collectibles
The Working Folding Knife
The Lore of Spices

FIREARMS
Antique Guns
P-38 Automatic Pistol
The Walther Handgun Story
Complete Guide to
  Compact Handguns
Complete Guide to Service Handguns
America's Great Gunmakers
Firearms Disassembly
  with Exploded Views
Rifle Guide
Gunsmithing at Home
The Book of the Twenty-Two
Complete Guide to Modern Rifles
Complete Guide to Classic Rifles
Legendary Sporting Rifles
FN Browning Armorer to the World
Modern Beretta Firearms
How to Buy & Sell Used Guns
Heckler & Koch:
  Armorers of the Free World
Spanish Handguns

RELOADING
The Handloader's Manual of
  Cartridge Conversions
Modern Sporting Rifle Cartridges
Complete Reloading Guide

FISHING
Ultimate Bass Boats
Bassing Bible
The Flytier's Companion
Deceiving Trout
The Complete Book of Trout Fishing
The Complete Book of Flyfishing
Peter Dean's Guide to Fly-Tying
The Flytier's Manual
Flytier's Master Class
Handbook of Fly Tying
The Fly Fisherman's Entomological
  Pattern Book
Fiberglass Rod Making
To Rise a Trout

MOTORCYCLES & TRUCKS
The Legend of Harley-Davidson
The Legend of the Indian
Best of Harley-Davidson
Classic Bikes
Great Trucks
4X4 Vehicles

COOKING GAME
Fish & Shellfish Care & Cookery
Game Cookbook
Dress 'Em Out
Wild About Venison
Wild About Game Birds
Wild About Freshwater Fish

PHOTOGRAPHY CREDITS
Paul T. Brown: Cover (2), 3, 62-63, 142-143, 155; Jay T. Langston:
34, 90-91; Alex Bowers: 79; Tom Evans: 139, 146-147.

HUNTING WHITETAILS
East & West

by J. Wayne Fears
and Larry Weishuhn

STOEGER PUBLISHING COMPANY, ACCOKEEK, MARYLAND

As deer hunters, we all know the mind games we occasionally need to play. You're hunting a stand with true potential for a tremendous buck. You've done the research, covered the miles, been patient in waiting for the right day and the right wind. Yet the morning drags on with no buck. These hours and the patience you muster will be the difference between success and another "...well, there's always next year" kind of season.

So to keep yourself in the stand and your senses alert, you perform mental gymnastics. One of my personal favorites is inventorying the gear I'd want if I were stranded in a remote camp. Used to be that this game would spin off into figuring out the best companions with whom to face such a predicament. Being there with tolerable company would be at least as important as the right gear.

Today, this game doesn't hold my attention anymore. I know, without a doubt, the two hunters with whom I'd want to share that weather-bound camp. Heck, with these guys there, I'd have to be crazy to want to go home!

The authors of this book, J. Wayne Fears and Larry Weishuhn, are those hunters and would-be campmates. Besides being outdoorsmen who know how to survive and thrive in the woods, any hunter could learn volumes on game and its ways from these men. Both have decades of experience as trained biologists and land managers. And they've spent even more time pursuing deer in every North American terrain and locale. If there's a hunting technique or strategy that's been tried or even thought about, this pair has already come across it and probably improved on it. Only years and miles and unwavering focus could gather the information in this book. These two are about the only ones around today who could have written it!

How do I know Wayne and Larry are the hunters with whom I'd want to be stranded more than any others? We've been there together. Wayne and I waited out blizzards and 60-below temperature to bump for miles over the tundra in pursuit of muskox and Perry caribou. Larry was with me in the blind when I went from steely-nerved killer to hyperventilating basket case in the split second I took aim at my first whitetail with a handgun.

With Dad enjoying hunts in the beyond, there are no better hunting companions left in this world.

Bill Miller
A grateful friend and campmate

We love hunting white-tailed deer! Throughout our life, deer have provided us with a vocation, an avocation, and often great inspiration. Having sampled a fair portion of the world's big-game hunting, we have never found a more challenging, interesting, adaptable, ever-changing, fun to hunt, and sometimes downright aggravating big game animal to pursue than our native white-tailed deer.

ardwoods or evergreen forests, open and broken ridges, ragged foothills, sunflower-studded prairies, expansive fields of corn and soybeans, narrow hardwoods, creek bottoms, large clear-cuts, dank swamp and marshes, arid desert lands of cactus and thornbush, these and many variations thereof comprise ideal white-tailed deer habitat.

The whitetail is America's deer! Only two states do not have white-tailed deer living freely within their boundaries. They are found throughout southern Canada. Not only has the whitetail learned to adapt to many types of habitat and terrain they, particularly mature bucks, learned how to quite often successfully evade human predators. That is one of the reasons they are so universally appealing to hunters.

Mature bucks and does, where they have survived hunting pressure, are practically "a breed apart" when compared to immature deer. Mature bucks provide hunting challenges unlike any found throughout the rest of the world. Everyone who has hunted regal red stag throughout the world or Africa's greater kudu tends to compare the "game of kings" to the wiles of a white-tailed deer. Yet, all but a few individual bulls and stags fail in comparison when it comes to the evasive behavior of mature whitetails who have survived several hunting seasons.

In terms of worldly deer hunting interest, perhaps only the diminutive roe deer of Europe has gained a cult following such as white-tailed deer have in North America. Quite frankly, there are many more whitetail hunters in the world than there are roe deer hunters.

The white-tailed deer regardless of where his kind lives may look quite similar, other than body size and hair coat that is basically dictated by climate, but they do not always behave in a similar manner. To a great extent, habitat dictates how a whitetail behaves and reacts when presented with perceived or real danger. However, never forget deer are individuals. They are not all stamped from the same mold.

No two whitetail racks are exactly the same. The same thing can be said of the deer themselves. As individuals, as well as a species, they adapt to their surroundings to survive. This is a lesson we learned as we matured as deer hunters. Their ability to adapt to their varied habitats is part of the grand appeal and interest in hunting their kind in different types of terrain throughout North America.

Each of us grew up in a different part of rural America, Weishuhn in the southern part of Texas in the gravel hills just north of the Gulf Coast prairie, Fears in the hardwood foothills of northern Alabama. While hundreds of miles apart, our little rural communities had a lot in common, as they were

The East can offer the whitetail hunter a variety of terrain but thickly grown and forested habitats are normal.

comprised of deer hunters whose ancestors had depended upon white-tailed deer and other game and fish to survive. During Weishuhn's early years, they hunted deer even though at the time whitetail populations were quite scarce. Where Fears grew up there were no deer remaining and hunters had to travel to go deer hunting. If someone in either community took a deer, he or she was regarded as a hero.

During our early teen years, each of us spent many hours dreaming of becoming a successful deer hunter. We read everything we could about whitetail hunting. We also fondly remember sitting around a campfire absorbing every word of the deer hunting stories told by our dads and their friends.

As youngsters, our whole world revolved around guns, hunting, and white-tailed deer. Come to think of it, not a whole lot has changed in our lives other than perhaps the fact that these days we travel throughout North America pursuing whitetails, rather than simply hunt the woods and fields behind the homes where we were reared.

Hunting the woods, tall timber bottoms, and the dense deciduous forests of the eastern half of

Years of hard-won experience at surviving hunting pressure makes mature bucks, such as this eastern, B&C 170-class ten-pointer, truly a breed apart.

North America provides many different challenges, especially to someone who has spent considerable time hunting the more open deer habitats of the West. Put Weishuhn in a wood lot on the eastern side of the continent and he starts feeling a bit claustrophobic. Put Fears on an open plain and he starts looking for a tree to use as a shooting support.

Hunting these areas provides great challenges and causes us to totally reevaluate our hunting schemes. In the eastern areas, there is quite often a distinct difference between bedding and feeding areas. Often these are separated by substantial distances. The same may be true in limited western areas, but certainly not true in many areas of the Southwest. In the arid brush country of southern Texas and northern Mexico, the distance between feeding and bedding areas may only be a matter of inches. Often they are one and the same.

Advice given about where to hunt in the East may revolve around such fall/winter food supplies as honeysuckle, smilax, and other wintergreen vines or even apples or other orchard fruit. Such food items do not exist throughout much of the whitetail's western habitat.

As someone who has often guided hunters from the East on their first western whitetail hunt, Weishuhn has quite frequently smiled at their reaction when they first see prime Texas or the western reaches of the Great Plains whitetail habitat. True to the bone, Pennsylvania, New Hampshire, New York, and other eastern states' hunters often stare in

disbelief of the habitats in which they are expected to hunt western whitetails. On the other hand, Fears has seen western hunters shake their heads in disbelief when he has guided them into thick eastern river bottom swamps. They were more concerned about snakes than big deer.

We realize with the advent of television shows and videos, whitetail hunters these days have a better understanding of what to expect if they journey to the East from the West and vice versa. However, until you've experienced firsthand the different types of habitats yourself, you can't appreciate the difference.

We have been extremely fortunate to be outdoor writers/wildlife professionals who have long special-

Hunting mature whitetail bucks in the more open terrain of the West offers greater opportunities for long-range shots.

J. WAYNE FEARS

LARRY WEISHUHN

ized in white-tailed deer. We have been privileged to hunt whitetails throughout North America. We truly look forward to hunting new territory on both sides of the Mississippi and view each hunt as a great new challenge.

Long before making the hunt we spend time learning all we can about the terrain we are going to hunt, weather conditions to expect, trying to determine what food sources the deer might be feeding on when we'll be in the area, learning all we can about what activities the deer will be involved in while we are there. Will the rut be beginning, in full swing, or finished for the year?

We'll make every effort to learn as much about the terrain as possible by procuring a map, either one commercially available or perhaps one we can get from someone who has previously hunted the area. If it's a guided or semi-guided hunt, we'll want to learn all we can from the guide and be able to garner from his experiences those gems which might help us to be successful.

We hope that we will be able to provide a few of those gems here in our book to make your hunt more successful, regardless of which side of the Mississippi you hunt! Weishuhn will take the western half of the country and Fears will take the eastern half. Together we will share our more than a century of whitetail hunting experience with you.

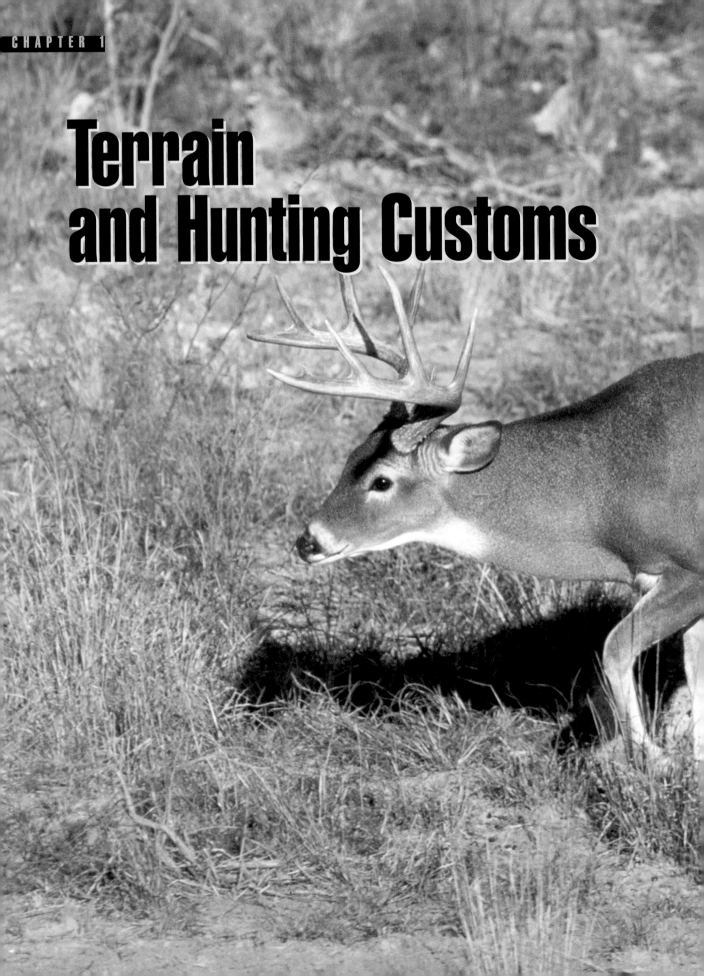

Terrain and Hunting Customs

Head down, a 160 B&C whitetail buck sneaks through mesquite and cactus in South Texas. North American whitetails range from northeastern deciduous forests to western shrub and mesquite creek bottoms.

East

One of the great things about hunting the white-tailed deer is that all you have to do to get a new adventure is to go a few miles up or down the road and the terrain, and most likely the traditional way of hunting will be different. Even in the same state, the method of hunting and the type of habitat you will be hunting will change drastically. To put an interesting spin on the hunt, the deer habitats will often be different.

Several years ago when I lived in South Carolina, I started the deer season in August hunting deer in hot, thick, swamps. Hunting was done by sitting on a stand along logging roads and letting dogs push the deer past hunters. Later in the season, I hunted in a county in the central part of the state where the terrain was rolling hills of pine/hardwood mixed forest. Here most hunting was from elevated stands along the edges of food plots planted for deer. Then late in the season I stalk-hunted deer in the steep mountainous northwestern corner of the state. Each of these hunts was entirely different. Each required a different dress, gear, and firearms. Each involved a different method of hunting and the deer had different habits. The hunting customs in each camp were different. It made a fun and challenging hunting season.

I think, if we would admit it, some of the most fun we have deer hunting is the planning and anticipation of the hunt. Because of this, the vast changes of terrain and hunting customs found in the eastern half of North America can make white-tailed deer hunting a lifetime sport that will never be boring.

Many of my whitetail hunts to different regions have been years in the planning and some were dream trips that I was never sure I would ever actually take. However, it was a fun and learning experience to read all I could about the area and how the local hunters hunted it. I enjoyed, and still do, studying about the terrain, weather, deer habitats, rutting dates, and season opening/closing dates. I especially like learning hunting techniques that local hunters have developed to hunt the deer in their area. Just when I think I have seen it all, I hunt an area where the local technique is totally new to me, and it works.

While it would take a series of books to examine all the various eastern habitats and hunting methods, let's look at a sample of what is out there for today's hunter.

THE SNOW BELT

When I first went to the state of Maine to hunt I was amazed at the habitat and terrain diversity one can hunt in one day. There were steep mountains and wet bottomland. There were thick forests, filled with blowdowns, and there were open clear-cuts. Most of all there was snow, lots of snow.

Perhaps what surprised me the most was the low population density of white-tailed deer. I had always thought there were lots of deer in Maine but by southern standards, there are not. Figuring out how to hunt this area was a mystery to me.

One of the first hunting methods I was introduced to up there is one that I have seen used throughout the Snow Belt around the Great Lakes. It can best be called tracking. It requires a lot of knowledge about the terrain being hunted, skills of a master woodsman, stamina, and an understanding of the habitats and habits of bucks. However, it works.

Tracking is done when there is snow on the ground. The experienced tracker looks for fresh tracks. He will study the tracks for a distance, taking into consideration how the animal moves, his stride, the size of the track, and other signs. If he determines he is on the fresh track of a big buck, he will set off after him. It is not a race but a form of stalk hunting that may go on for miles. Those who have the skills and stamina to follow a buck cross-country find this method of hunting ideal for the Snow Belt. The Benoit family of Vermont has become famous in hunting circles for developing this hunting method. Now their green plaid hunting coats and pump-action rifles have become the "trademark" of this method of hunting. It has spread throughout the northern Snow Belt.

Tracking whitetails in a New England snow requires the endurance and skills of a master woodsman.

THE FARM BELT

Middle America is known as the Corn Belt but along the Ohio River region and beyond there is some of the country's best white-tailed deer hunting on small farms, which dot this landscape. These deer are well fed and often their home range is small. With plenty of nutritious food handy and does that are handy, there is little reason for them to roam. I have met hunters who told me they have hunted a buck that spent the entire season in one cornfield. Bucks that hold up tight like this offer the hunter a challenge.

Where legal, small man drives are used to push bucks out into the open in this type of country. Several years ago I was on a well-organized man drive near the Ohio River. It was a sweeping drive that had a pivot

A well-organized drive can produce elusive bucks from their hiding places in large plots of standing corn.

Hunting from a stand is used extensively in the forested slopes and valleys of the Appalachian Mountains.

where a cornfield cornered with a pasture. I had the pivot position and would stay in the fence corner while the other drivers walked through the standing corn to the fence that separated the cornfield from the pasture. It was cold and I used the large corner post to block off the wind. As the other hunters walked through the corn, I saw two does leave the safety of the corn and run across the pasture. This was encouraging. Soon I saw a hunter appear at the far end of the fencerow and I knew the drive was about over. At about the same time I heard a sound of something coming through the corn just to my left. I thought it might be one of the other hunters who had gotten off course. I squatted down and looked under the corn leaves to see the lower half of a deer coming straight to the corner where I was standing. I got my shotgun ready. The deer passed just behind me and into a thick fencerow to my right.

There he felt safe and stopped to look back at the cornfield. It was the break I needed. The rifled slug found its mark. The short man drive produced two bucks in terrain that would have been almost impossible to hunt any other way.

A farm family I hunt with in Illinois stand hunts the narrow wooded corridors that run along the fencerows that separate their fields. This is one of the best hunting techniques for several situations and will be covered in detail later in this book so I won't discuss it here other than to say it is a most successful way to hunt farm country.

APPALACHIAN MOUNTAINS

The backbone of the eastern half of the country is the Appalachian Mountains. Here the carrying capacity for deer is lower so there are fewer deer to hunt. The hunt is challenging and it is one of my favorite areas to hunt. There is something about trying to outsmart the bucks found in this region of steep, hardwood ridges and thick laurel-covered hollows that bring out my Scotch-Irish and Cherokee ancestry. In fact, my farm in Alabama is located in the southern end of the Appalachians.

Hunting methods for this area vary from scrape hunters who sit on fresh scrapes found on ridge tops or in bottoms to long-range shooters who locate heavily used trails on the side of a ridge and take a stand on an opposite ridge.

Some years the best method for this area is the location of a food source and to stake it out. Food for white-tailed deer in these mountains can be scarce some years. When that is the case, it works to the hunter's benefit. Find an old homeplace grown up in honeysuckle, a remote white oak full of acorns, or a small mountain farm with winter wheat planted as temporary pasture and you will find deer.

Hunting these mountains can be very physical, especially when you get a deer down in the bottom of some remote hollow, but it can be a very rewarding hunt and one reminiscent of our forefathers' time. I like these mountain hunts where a tent camp is the base camp and muzzleloading rifles add just the right touch to the experience.

SOUTHERN MIXED HARDWOODS/PINE FOREST

The South is blessed with a higher carrying capacity and thus a denser deer population. Due to this, many of the southern states have a long deer season and liberal bag limits. Hunting here has changed a lot over the last three decades. Once dogs were used extensively to drive deer from thick swamps and brush into the open, allowing hunters to get a shot at a buck. However, this has changed and now still-hunting has become the most popular and successful technique used.

The tremendous growth in the number of hunting clubs leasing land for their members to hunt on has given many hunters a private place to learn and to hunt season after season. By getting to know the land and learning the deer habitats on that land, hunters have become more skilled at selecting stand sites and having the opportunity to sit on those stands longer. It is paying off in bucks taken.

By the same token, many hunters who hunt public hunting areas have hunted the areas for many seasons and take the time to scout and select good stand sites before opening day. This is not to say that there are no stalk hunters or dog drive hunters for there are, but stand hunting has become very common in the South and seems to be growing each year.

Regardless of where you hunt in the East, you would be wise to listen to the local hunters and learn from their experience as to the hunting technique you use, the clothing and gear you select to use, and the firearm and load you bring. Their reasons for their choices are usually good.

I am often entertained by the reaction of a guest hunter when I tell him to come to the South

The use of a portable tree stand is one of the most successful ways to hunt in the South's overgrown mixed hardwood and pine forests.

dressed in layers to stay warm and he reminds me we southerners don't know what cold is. Two famous hunters, Glenn Helgeland of Wisconsin and Jay Verzuh of Colorado laughed at me when I told them it would be cold hunting deer with me in Alabama in December. Each will tell you now that the coldest they have ever been was hunting with Fears in Alabama. The 100 percent humidity at 19 degrees will get

you no matter how cold it gets where you live.

The point is there is some great deer hunting throughout the East, just adapt to the terrain, weather, and deer habits, and you will find the changes a fun challenge. Look at deer hunting as a sport for life. It is a work in progress as we are always a student; and in the end, we won't know it all, but the process of learning is about as much fun as a person can have.

West

Those hunters faced with hunting western white-tailed deer for the first time, having previously never even seen western habitats, must undoubtedly think, "No way! There cannot be any white-tailed deer in this country because there's no place to hide. Besides, what is there for them to eat? No oaks, no beech, nor even honeysuckle vines. Surely no self-respecting whitetails would live here!"

I recall hunting clients making such comments when confronted with the mesquite and cactus country of southern Texas. This was before the advent of videos and the proliferation of outdoor television shows which frequently did their programs from southern Texas. During the early days, many eastern hunters had only read about South Texas's "muy grande" bucks.

They would arrive, take one look at the low-growing brush and cactus, and think themselves had. But by the time their guided hunts were over, they had seen more and better white-tailed bucks in those few days hunting South Texas than they had previously seen in over 20 years of hunting the densely wooded areas of Pennsylvania and other eastern prime hunting destinations.

Our biggest "problem" as guides was preventing clients from wanting to shoot the first eight-point buck they saw. It was not easy keeping them from shooting a lesser buck than they would otherwise be capable of taking if they exercised a bit of restraint and patience. Quite often, they would shoot the first eight-point buck they saw, only to see a lot of much larger bucks. But then, many of those hunters had never before seen an eight-point buck, and their goal in life was to simply take a buck with eight total points.

WESTERN HABITATS

Western white-tailed deer habitat and terrain varies from extremely flat to grassy plains to rolling hills to high mountains to dense arboreal forests to great expanses of farmland traversed by small creek bottoms and drainages. Deer habitat is relative to the immediate area. There really isn't any classic western deer habitat like could be said of eastern white oak ridges. Western white-tailed deer habitat comes in many forms. Bedding and feeding areas are often measured as being apart by mere inches, if at all separated.

In southern Texas the difference between "creek bottom" and "upland" habitat is often measured only in the relative height of mesquite trees. Other shrub-type and cactus vegetation may be similar throughout. On South Texas and northern Mexico upland habitat mesquite trees may grow to be 6 to 10 feet tall. In "creek bottom" habitat, they may grow 12 to 14 feet tall.

DEER FOODS

The difference between good and not so good deer habitat is often measured in terms of annual precipitation. With adequate rainfall, say between 12 and 16 inches annually, much western terrain can grow a tremendous amount of forbs or weeds, ideal deer food. Quite often, the timeliness of the precipitation is of equal if not more importance than the total amount received. Late fall and winter rains grow great amounts of forbs not only for winter feed but also for early spring feed. Forbs as a group are highly nutritious and are extremely important not only in the arid Southwest but throughout their entire western range.

Stress periods for western whitetails are late summer, because of heat and a lack of rainfall, and late winter, whereas in the southern portion a lack of rainfall causes great stress due to a lack of food, or because of extremely harsh winters in the northern portions.

In the southern portion of the West, mast crops come primarily in the form of mesquite beans which are high in sucrose and energy. Prickly pear fruit, locally called "tunas," are also an important energy source. Cactus, especially the various species of prickly pear, provides moisture and food during both good and bad times. Since oak and other mast-bearing trees are sparse in many areas of the West, deer depend to a great degree upon these two primary "mast" crops. In other parts of the Southwest, low-growing oaks tend to produce sporadic acorn crops.

Heading northward and westward into the famed Texas Hill Country there are rough and rolling hills. These are often covered with juniper and a wide variety of low-growing oak trees, as well as other relatively low-growing trees and shrubs. Western oaks tend to produce substantial mast crops only occasionally, usually once every three or four years.

Western habitats are changing, thankfully!

A LESSON LEARNED

The Texas Hill Country was once an area of extremes in terms of deer densities and body sizes. Back in the mid-1950s through 1960s it was not uncommon for range conditions to deteriorate to the point of thousands of whitetails starving to death. This situation was complicated by overpopulations of whitetails, and overutilization by both domestic stock and whitetails themselves.

During the late 1960s, as a "new" biologist with the state of Texas, I conducted dead deer surveys to determine the severity of local die-offs. Back then, too, it was not uncommon to weigh mature hunter-harvested bucks that field-dressed 60 to 70 pounds.

Thankfully these extensive deer die-offs no longer occur thanks to the acceptance and implantation of modern wildlife management techniques. Today in those same areas it is not uncommon for mature bucks to field-dress 120 to 140 or more pounds.

Overgrazing by livestock is bad for the climax vegetation. Past overgrazing by cattle, horses, sheep, and goats has created great biodiversity and certainly had a hand in increasing whitetail populations.

The Great Plains, from the Mississippi River westward to the foothills of the Rocky Mountains, was once a huge sea of grass populated primarily by buffalo, elk, pronghorn antelope, and mule deer. White-tailed deer, sometimes called "common deer" during early exploration days were restricted primarily to the drainages. Whitetails existed throughout much of the West during early historic times, but not necessarily in great numbers. That too has changed.

During the early years, whitetails were often marketed hunted until their numbers were extremely low. Thankfully things changed.

Previous grasslands changed from being primarily grazed by livestock to small farms. These planted crops provided more year-round nutrition for whitetails and their numbers increased.

Unfortunately in some western areas where both whitetails and mule deer coexisted, ranchers shot the whitetails because they were concerned the two would interbreed and the integrity of the mule deer would be destroyed. Little did they realize, while there is some interbreeding that occurs wherever the two species exist, these crossing did not create sterile offspring. They simply looked more like their dam than their sire.

In far western Texas where both desert mule deer and the local whitetail subspecies of whitetails live, the Carmen Mountains whitetail (arguably the smallest whitetail subspecies) was shot extensively to keep the two from interbreeding or taking over the range. What was not realized is that the two exist in excellent harmony and occupy two different habitats. In the Big Bend Area of Texas the Carmen Mountains whitetail exist at elevations above 4,500 feet. Desert mule deer live below that level.

WESTERN WHITETAIL NUMBERS EXPAND

But throughout much of the West the whitetail has been seen as an invader. Only with the current great interest in whitetails have opinions changed.

Not only have whitetail numbers increased due to changes in agriculture, their numbers also increased because of aggressive trapping and transplanting projects undertaken by state wildlife or "game" departments or agencies.

During the first half of the 1900s thousands of white-tailed deer were trapped in such places as Texas and then shipped and released in many different areas of the country. In the Midwest, whitetails were reestablished in areas from which they had long been removed, primarily because of habitat destruction and market hunting. Whitetails were also introduced into habitats previously unoccupied by their kind during at least recent history.

As whitetail populations increased there was also "natural movement" into many of the western habitats. There is an innate sense in some animals as it is in humans to explore and populate previously unoccupied areas. This too has contributed to the westward expansions of whitetails.

The whitetail is a survivor and can adapt to a wide variety of habitats and terrain.

Farther north and west in such states as Montana, Idaho, and Washington the whitetail learned to adapt to the foothills and to great expanses of timbered mountains, ridges, and drainages. The same has long been true in the Provincial Forest of the western Canadian Provinces.

On a recent Rocky Mountain goat and elk hunting trip into the famed Prophet and Muskwa River areas of British Columbia, I saw several whitetails in creek and river bottoms fed by glaciers. I suspect in time they will adapt and reach even the high peaks just below the glaciers. In these more remote areas the expansion of the whitetail has been a natural occurrence.

In other areas of Canada, as in a goodly portion of the United States, white-tailed deer have expanded their range and especially their populations due to

Larry Weishuhn scouts a rugged creek bottom in Texas. In the West white-tailed deer habitat comes in many forms.

the increase in agriculture. Grassland prairies produce a very limited amount of deer food. Huge corn, soybean, milo, various legumes, and similar crops produce a great amount of high-quality deer foods. These factors along with favorable weather conditions have led to the westward, northern and possibly southern expansion of white-tailed deer.

HUNTING TRADITIONS

Whitetails have been an "interesting" animal in the West when it comes to hunting traditions. In the northern regions of the West, especially where both mule deer and whitetails coexist, many hunters in years past did not "bother" hunting whitetails, not until the whitetail craze began in the mid-1970s and early 1980s. Mule deer were easier to hunt and easier to come by throughout much of the West.

In areas of the Midwest back at the turn of the 20th century there were few whitetails left. Their numbers did not increase to huntable populations until about the 1960s. Many states had closed season on deer.

In the Southwest where I grew up people hunted deer prior to the 1960s even when deer numbers and hunter success were relatively low. It wasn't until the extinction of the screwworm fly that deer populations increased over much of Texas. In southern Texas, ranches were of huge acreages and access was generally limited to family and a few close friends.

Then in the late 1960s things started changing, as did hunting regulations. In Texas the Game Department started encouraging the taking of does. These requests were initially met with great opposition from both landowners/mangers and hunters. The 1970s saw emphasis being placed on quality in terms of antlers and bodies and efforts were begun to bring deer quality back to where it had been when

populations were lower and food was more abundant. About this time John Wootters started writing about trophy deer. Approximately the same time Jerry Smith started photographing big, mature whitetails. Those photos started appearing in magazines and on covers. Wootters' writings soon became a book, *Hunting Trophy Deer*. During the middle 1970s two biologists from Texas, Al Brothers and Murphy Ray, started doing seminars about producing quality deer herds. Those seminars were quickly turned into the bible for the deer manager/hunter, *Producing Quality Whitetails*. At that point things began to change drastically and considerably quicker than ever before. Whitetail mania had begun and soon America's deer had a cult following of momentous proportions.

Hunting traditions seemed to change with the trends in deer populations and management. When I was a youngster during the 1950s and early 1960s practically everyone in our rural Zimmerscheidt community hunted deer. November 16 was the opening date. If employers did not grant their employees the day off, they called in sick. Still others quit their jobs so they could hunt.

In our family my mother Lillie, dad Lester, my brother Glenn, and I all hunted whitetails. The first week of the season we moved to our "camp house," a one-room tin building about 500 yards behind our home. Not only did we hunt every day that first week, most evenings we entertained other hunters. Friends and relatives from throughout the community stopped by camp to show off deer and talk about the ones that got away. Our soup and coffeepots were always "on."

Our camp was no different than others in the area. Men, women, and children hunted deer. Like our family they often moved to deer camp during a goodly portion of the six-week-long season. Today, even though the "hunter structure" has changed, the tradition of hunting whitetails lives on.

In years past I frequently visited with my dad and some of his cohorts about what deer hunting was like when they were young men during the late 1920s and 1930s. According to them, men in Model A's, Model T's and even horse-drawn wagons would arrive and begin setting up camp on land belonging to my granddad and great-granddad several days before the season opened. Lean-tos were erected for kitchen and sleeping quarters. Often there were as many as 20 hunters in camp. The successful deer hunter would blow a horn fashioned from a cow horn to signal his success to all within hearing.

According to him, these were traditional camps that had been set up each year as far back as those attending could remember, and several back then were in their 60s and 70s. Those camps must have been quite a sight.

In time things started changing and no longer did landowners allow just anyone to hunt their properties. The same was happening elsewhere. Times got better after World War II and city and country dwellers alike had more money to spend. They started offering landowners money for the exclusive rights to hunt their properties.

Hunting traditions continue, even if slightly different than before.

Predawn customers crowd a western "quick-mart" during whitetail season.

The guns today's hunters carry and the clothes they wear may be different from those hunters of yore, but the desire and tradition of deer hunting remain much the same.

White-tailed deer hunting season is a major occurrence throughout many of the western states. Even today one frequently sees banners stretched across highways on the edge of small towns and cities stating, "HUNTERS WELCOME." Many towns and communities also provide special meals and entertainment to visiting hunters on the night before the season opens. A considerable number of rural communities and towns, not only in Texas but throughout the West, would have little, if any, income were it not for the visiting hunters. Landowners in many western areas have come to depend heavily upon lease money from hunters. This "deer lease money" goes a long way to paying taxes and quite often provides the farmer's or rancher's only stable income for the year.

Some hunters with money to spend buy their own property to manage and hunt. This is more than simply a trend, it's becoming the norm. Most of the land sold throughout the West is being bought for recreational purposes. The times are changing, but thankfully the hunting tradition continues.

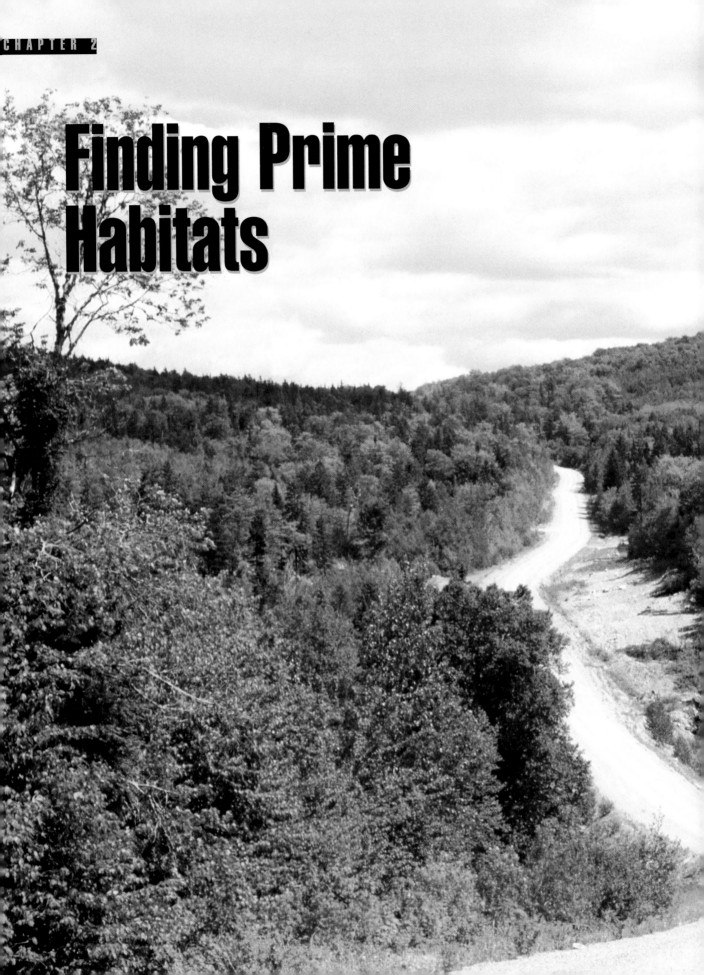

Finding Prime Habitats

Dense cover of young cutover vegetation flanks a dirt road in a stretch of reforested land. Much of the eastern half of North America is prime whitetail habitat.

East

"You are so lucky," is the comment you will hear repeatedly when the casual deer hunter visits the trophy room of a deer hunter who takes good bucks, year after year. Yes, luck may play a role in taking one exceptional buck but the hunter who takes big bucks regularly counts on more than luck, he knows how to find prime deer habitat wherever he hunts and how to hunt it.

The eastern half of North America is dotted with pockets of prime white-tailed deer habitat; learn how to find them, and that is where you will find the best bucks. Since eastern deer have much smaller home ranges than their western cousins, bucks in these prime habitats can be somewhat easier to find.

While this sounds easy, there are changes taking place on or near these prime habitats that keep many of them in a state of change. Examples would include the expansion of human development, changes in forestry and land management, weather extremes, natural plant succession, and increasing deer population density. Any of these can destroy a prime deer habitat, and in some cases, create a new one. The secret is to be able to recognize a current prime habitat and hunt it while it is still prime.

On one of my many hunts with Realtree founder Bill Jordan, we were hunting a large tract of land in Georgia that had once been covered in small farms. Now the land is in a long-term forest management program. Not being familiar with the property, I discussed the lay of the land with the land manager. As we talked, I kept asking questions about key factors that would direct me to prime habitat. His answers told me that a particular hollow, which had once been a homestead, would be an ideal place to hunt.

The first day of the hunt, I was told by the hunt manager to hunt a stand that overlooked a power line right-of-way. During the day, I saw several deer and that afternoon took a nine-point buck. Since there was a two-buck limit on the area, I was allowed to hunt the next day.

That night I asked Bill about hunting the hollow the land manager had told me about. Bill gave his okay, with the warning there were no stands in the hollow, and no one had hunted in there, so it may not be good hunting. I told him I would take my chances.

The next morning Bill dropped me off at the head of the hollow and said, I would be picked up at 11:00. I waited until daylight and made my way down the hollow until I found the site where a small farmhouse had once been. There I found the keys to prime habitat and lots of fresh scrapes. I got on a ridge where I could see down into the hollow and got comfortable. As soon as I got still I began to see does. Around 8:00 I saw a wide ten-point buck ease out of a grown-over ridge top opposite where I was sitting and start down into the hollow. He stopped at a scrape some 120 yards from my position and started pawing the earth. The little 7X57 Ruger No. 1 came up and the buck went down. He never twitched.

Since this was such a prime area and I had a lot of time to field-dress the buck I unloaded my rifle and decided to sit and watch the hollow for a while. Soon things got back to normal and a doe and fawn walked within 20 feet of me. A short time later, I saw a movement in the sunshine down the hollow. Here came a much larger ten-point buck. If only I had waited, but I had a good buck. He walked up to my fallen buck, sniffed him, and then sniffed the scrape. Slowly he rubbed his face on the overhanging limb, licked it, and walked away.

What a morning! Hunting prime habitat paid off. The wide ten-point buck is on my wall now to remind me of that exciting morning.

KEYS TO PRIME EASTERN DEER HABITAT

Whether you are interested in managing a hunting club for large deer or want to hunt the best possible locations for deer, knowing the keys to prime habitat is a must. They will vary somewhat in the East by geographical regions but these guidelines will help you know what to look for when scouting or selecting a place to hunt.

Bill Jordan (right) congratulates Wayne Fears on taking this ten-pointer in a prime tract of Georgia woodland.

CARRYING CAPACITY – If the area is overpopulated with deer, then chances are good there will not be any prime habitat to hunt. Prime habitat is found in areas where deer populations are within the carrying capacity of the land. I like areas where the deer population is under the carrying capacity. That means there is more nutritious food for the deer to eat, the antlers on mature bucks are larger, and the number of does is lower causing the bucks to have to move around more during the rut.

SOIL FERTILITY – You can't have prime habitat without high soil fertility. Deer health is no better than the nutritional quality of the food they eat. In many areas of the East, the highest soil fertility is found along river and creek bottoms. In fact, in one study of large bucks taken in Georgia, 83 percent were taken close to major river systems. In addition, soil fertility is high in agricultural areas. Some of the best bucks being taken today come out of farm areas where crops that deer feed on are fertilized according to soil tests.

FOOD DIVERSITY – For deer to be healthy and for bucks to grow large antlers, there must be a diversity of food on a 12-month basis. Prime habitat offers lots of hard and soft mast, lots of high-quality browse, and in some cases access to agricultural crops. This is one of the reasons wildlife biologists encourage hunting clubs to plant their food plots in the spring as well as in the fall. A good food supply during one season and a poor one in another doesn't offer prime habitat.

COVER – Eastern deer require cover for bedding areas, winter yarding, escape, fawning, and movement. The prime deer habitat will include thick areas that offer deer protection and safe corridors to move about. Prime deer habitat will include lots of edges, forest of different age classes of trees, and broken openings.

WATER – Fortunately the East is blessed with a lot of water and most habitats offer plenty of water. However, drought can take a prime habitat and reduce it to a poor habitat. In the Southeast one of the most stressful periods for deer is late summer and early fall. There is less soil moisture and when combined with high temperatures the quality of the vegetation they eat is poor. Throw a drought in this

period and the habitat and the deer are in trouble.

WEATHER – Floods, heavy snowfall, late freezes, and droughts can all reduce the quality of habitat. Take a year where the mast crop is poor due to a drought or late freeze and then have a hard winter and the deer and habitat suffer. Deep snow brings on winter stress to northern deer and when this occurs, their habitat also suffers from overbrowsing and hard freezes.

While there is little we can do about the weather, it should be a consideration if you are planning on going to an area to hunt deer. While looking for prime habitats you should ask about the past year's weather.

PRIME HABITATS MAY BE FOUND ANYWHERE

There are pockets of prime habitat found in all sections of the East. You just have to seek them out or create them if you are involved in managing land. The changes in clear-cutting policy in forests the past few years have created many small pockets of prime habitat. Now most forest cutting must leave timber, often mast producing hardwoods, standing along streams called streamside management zones (SMZ). As the forest starts to grow back, these SMZs become good pockets of deer habitat and great corridors to hunt.

I like to find old homesites back in the woods, such as the one I hunted at the beginning of this chapter. They usually offer thick cover where fields once grew, water at a spring or stream, mineral licks where the outhouse and smokehouse once stood, and a variety of foods ranging from soft mast from old fruit trees, remains of domestic plants, and possibly hard mast.

Agricultural areas that are broken up into diverse areas offer some of the best habitats found today. All the factors listed above may be found there, especially if the deer population has been kept within the carrying capacity.

I have hunted in southern New York where small dairies, broken up with dense fencerows and mast producing wood lots, offered deer the best of all worlds. Hard winters had kept the population down and these prime habitats were good hunting.

In addition, I have hunted in the Corn Belt where large fertile cornfields and the patchy woodlands found along fencerows and creeks provided the bucks with prime habitat. I must admit it took some effort to learn how to hunt these bucks but it is great fun.

PRIME HABITAT CAN BE CREATED

If you are involved in managing a family farm or hunting club lease, you can create your own prime habitat. It will take several years but the effort can be rewarded with great deer hunting.

Some 15 years ago, I purchased a rundown 300-acre farm in Alabama with the intention of creating prime deer and wild turkey habitat. I named it Cross Creek Hollow as you have to cross a creek to go anywhere on the farm. I began by writing a detailed wildlife management plan to keep me on tract over the years. I consulted with a soil survey obtained from the U.S. Natural Resource Conservation Service to determine where my best soils were. This is where I established my food plots.

Following the plan I established cover in the form of planted pines on the ridge tops. To increase hard mast production I planted several acres of fast-growing sawtooth oaks, selected, and annually fertilized white oak trees. Along the four creeks on the property, I allowed the alders to grow thick to offer deer lots of corridors for movement and escape. Some 20 acres of food plots are planted in the rich soil found in the creek bottoms. They are planted twice each year to keep a good supply of nutritious food. Selected natural growing plants such as honeysuckle, blackberry, blueberry, and smilax are fertilized each year.

We are in a quality deer management program which means that we have a prescribed number of does and only mature bucks annually to keep the deer population within the carrying capacity of the land. In short, we offer the deer everything they need in the way of prime habitat. The reward is great hunting for my family and friends.

Whether you create you own prime deer habitat for deer or seek it out for hunting in Vermont, Ohio, Kentucky, Florida or wherever, it is where you will find healthy deer and quite possibly that wall hanger you have been dreaming about.

LOCATING AREAS OF HIGH DEER NUMBERS

Not everyone is looking for a wall hanger. Those of us who enjoy the great taste of venison spend some time of each hunting season putting one or more deer in the freezer. In addition, those who are new to deer hunting need to hunt areas of high deer population densities to gain experience before going after a trophy. For all of these hunters are looking for areas where there are lots of deer, and the chance of bagging one is good.

Locating areas of high deer population density has never been easier. That information is as near as your computer. The Quality Deer Management Association (QDMA) has a U.S. White-Tailed Deer Density Map on its website, www.qdma.com. You can click on the state, then county, and then specific area and the map will give you the deer population density of that area.

One word of caution, do not let areas of high deer densities fool you; that it is easy hunting, or that you will see numbers of deer every day. I have lived and guided in areas of some of the highest deer densities in the world and there are days when you can't find a doe, much less a buck. I have seen deer disappear for up to five days at a time and the visiting hunter would question if there were any deer in the area. It is still hunting and you need to plan hunts into areas of high deer density just as you would for a trophy buck. The wind, weather, moon, etc., can cause deer to disappear in regions of the highest deer density.

A landowner disks a food plot to ensure a good supply of browse. Careful management can create prime habitat on a hunting lease or small farm.

West

The white-tailed deer is undoubtedly one of the most adaptable big game animals in the world, especially when it comes to human encroachment upon their habitat or in terms of agriculture. They can make themselves at home in a wood lot, or a literal forest of cornstalks, or within the city limits of major metropolises if given the slightest bit of cover. Thus, prime habitat comes in many forms including where it seldom rains, as is often the case within its western habitat.

The size and height of native vegetation is to a great extent determined by soil type and nutrients, the average annual precipitation, as well as by winter and summer temperature extremes. Throughout much of the whitetail's western habitat, annual rainfall rates are relatively low. Grasslands, savannah and shrub brush are the norm.

Arid land vegetation tends to protect itself with spines and thorns. Sharp thorns and spines discourage grazers and even some browsing animals from eating their leaves. This is especially true when it comes to grazers such as cattle. Cattle have a somewhat square muzzle. When a cow eats she somewhat indiscriminately wraps her tongue around vegetation and eats whatever grasses are pulled in.

Domestic sheep and goats and deer are ruminants like cattle. But they are more selective in what they eat. By nature's design their muzzle is somewhat pointed. This allows them to "reach in" and select only the most nutritious and palatable portions of the vegetation they browse.

LIVESTOCK, PLUSES AND MINUSES

Whereas cattle seldom compete with white-tailed deer for food, unless the range is extremely overgrazed, sheep and goats do compete with deer on a daily basis. This in the past has often created problems between domestic sheep and goats and deer. The result has generally been that deer considerations took a back seat to those of domestic livestock.

At one time sheep and goats were present and browsed much of the western deer range. This had both positive and negative results in light of whitetailed deer. The positive side of this was that while domestic sheep and goats were valuable, ranchers carried on an intensive predator control program, which in turn saved many a deer from being eaten by coyotes, bobcats, and cougars. When wool and mohair prices dropped sharply and they started switching over to cattle, they became lax in controlling predators and predation started taking its toll on deer, especially in certain areas of the West. The downside of domestic sheep and goat operations was the competition between livestock and deer for food. Before the value of wool and mohair decreased, ranges were often overstocked with domestic stock, and thus heavily competed with native white-tailed deer.

However, conditions and situations have changed throughout much of the West. In recent years the economic value of deer has become considerably higher than sheep and goats. As a result of ranchers switching to cattle grazing operations, the habitat in terms of browse availability and quality has improved. But, as mentioned, the downside is ranchers are no longer carrying on stringent predator control programs. Generally when it comes to deer and deer management, for every positive there is a negative and for every negative there is a positive.

Rainfall works much the same way. Where there is little annual precipitation there is not much water available, including for humans. Thus the lack of rainfall throughout much of the West's whitetail habitat is in one sense a negative because without much rain there is only limited vegetation and ground water. The positive side of this is, because there is little rainfall and little water, much of the western whitetail habitat has not been too seriously encroached upon by people and their changing land practices.

WESTERN VEGETATION

Good western whitetail habitat consists of a blend of vegetation, including both woody browse species and forbs. Mast crops of such trees as some of the western oaks do figure into the overall scheme of food availability, in some areas quite heavily and other areas not at all.

Most of the western woody browse can best be described as shrubs, meaning they are low-growing. The most nutritious and palatable portion of any browse is usually found at the top of the plant. In the case of shrubs, the tops of these plants are often at a height where a deer can reach them when browsing. This is unlike many of the eastern browse species which grow considerably taller than white-tailed deer can reach. To learn what deer eat in the particular area you live or plan on hunting, contact a local biologist employed by the state and discuss with him what deer in the particular area eat. He may also be able to suggest publications which not only tell you what deer in the area eat, but also how to identify those plants.

Western deer browse comes in many forms including such plants as various spiny hackberries, various sumacs, and many different species of acacia such as blackbrush, coma and many others. Many of the acacias and the various legumes, such as mesquite and other trees and shrubs produce "beans," but other than those of the mesquite tree these are not really eaten to a great extent by deer. The "beans" of other western shrubs, while not consumed by deer, are eaten by many of the regions' other wildlife, such as various species of squirrels, rats, and a great number of game and non-game birds.

As has been mentioned, cactus of many different species exist throughout much of the western deer habitat, with the exception of the Northwest. Deer

David Blanton tagged this 145 B&C buck on a Texas farm. Whitetails adapt easily to a wide range of habitats.

throughout the western half of the country utilize cactus throughout the year, and especially when the fruit or "tunas" ripen. These are favorites not only of white-tailed deer but also coyotes and even black bears, as well as many other species.

While in most instances the quality of western vegetation in terms of nutrients is generally fairly high, the abundance of browse is sometimes lacking. Deer populations throughout much of the West are relatively low, sometimes at a density of about one deer per 50 to 100 or more acres. There are certainly exceptions to this, and the higher deer densities are usually associated with crops such as the various cereal grains (wheat, oats, corn, milo and others). The number of deer an area can support depends to the greatest extent upon the available year-round food supply.

I've hunted areas of southern Texas and northern Mexico where the deer density was about one per 50 acres or even lower. I did not see many deer, but when I did see a buck he was certainly worth looking at. The same has been true for areas in Alberta and Saskatchewan, the total population was relatively low, but the quality in terms of antlers and body size was extremely good.

Texas in many ways has been a leader in deer production and management. This has been in part due to several factors, including most of the land in Texas is privately owned, landowners/managers there are extremely interested in quality deer, and rules and regulations regarding deer management have allowed private landowners/managers to more intensively manage their properties for deer.

FOOD PLOTS AND SUPPLEMENTAL FEEDING, NOTHING REALLY NEW

Food plots have become increasingly popular throughout much of the whitetail's range, including the western half of the North American continent. Food plots are actually nothing new when it comes to providing supplemental food for wildlife. Genghis Khan, many centuries ago, was responsible for the planting of food plots to increase game bird and other wildlife populations. He also was one of the first to provide supplemental feed for wildlife that existed on his properties. Europeans interested in red stags, roe deer, and chamois have been doing the same thing since before the time they even knew a

North American continent existed. Are food plots and supplemental feeding anything new? No, we have only modified some of the things done for centuries.

Many ranchers in Texas now provide supplemental feed in the form of pelleted rations to deer, yet in other states doing so is considered illegal. Why supplemental feed rather than food plots in the arid Southwest? The question almost answers itself. To grow crops you need basically two things, soil and water. The arid Southwest has soil, but water is a different matter. Throughout the eastern half of the continent rainfall is somewhat predictable and regularly occurring. Throughout much of the western half rainfall cannot be depended upon. Thus you can plant all the fancy seeds you want to, and if it doesn't rain they are not going to germinate, or worse yet it will rain just enough to germinate the food plot seeds and then quit. When that happens, you lose the entire crop you've planted.

While this is not the case throughout the entirety of the western half of North America, it is in a goodly portion. Thus, unlike what practices can be done to improve the deer habitat in the East does not necessarily work in the West.

Throughout the West the best that can normally be done to improve deer habitat is to carry on a good livestock grazing program, stocking domestic stock at numbers the range can support in the worst of times without putting undue grazing or browsing pressure on the land. The other important consideration is keeping the deer population and density "in tune" and at a level the range can support during the worst of times.

That said, there are certain areas of the West where the planting of food plots, especially with some of the legumes (clovers, vetches, and alfalfas) designed to withstand grazing pressure. When and where crops are planted, a portion of the crops can be left "standing" unharvested in the field to provide food for deer and other wildlife during the hard times of winter.

For a while I have been involved in the management of some property in eastern Colorado, in an area that has whitetails and mule deer, as well as elk and pronghorn antelope, all living upon the same property. The ranch has several pivot irrigation set-ups where alfalfa is planted. Each year those who hunt the property pay the rancher to leave a portion of the alfalfa in the fields for

Despite its desolate appearance, arid brush- and cactus-covered terrain, such as that encountered in these rugged hills in the American Southwest, can be productive for whitetails.

wildlife, rather than harvesting it for hay.

We have done similar things in western Iowa and similar habitats farther west where farmers grow corn and other row crops. Each year the hunters pay the farmer to leave a number of rows unharvested along the edges of creek bottoms, to provide food for the whitetails during the harshest part of winter.

Both these "situations" have worked extremely well for the deer and other wildlife, as well.

As a wildlife biologist long involved in western whitetail deer management I am often asked by those wishing to plant food plots to increase forage availability what they should plant. My answer seldom varies. "Go to farmers in the area where you want to plant something. Ask them what they plant that they have the most problem with when it comes to crop damage and loss from deer. Then plant it." By doing

so you are planting first of all, something you already know will grow in your area. You're also planting something that deer know what it is and they like it.

If you're going to be more adventurous, plant several strips of different types of "deer forage seeds." Then determine which of the plants grow in that particular area. Follow this with paying attention to what the deer prefer to eat. If it grows in your area, and deer eat it, plant more of it.

Another consideration in planting food plots, be it in the East or the West, is planting blends of seeds, so that some mature quicker than others. That way by planting a blend you will provide deer with variety (which they truly prefer) and forages that grow not only at different levels but at slightly different times.

Prime whitetail habitat comes in many forms. Never dismiss brush and cactus as being unproductive.

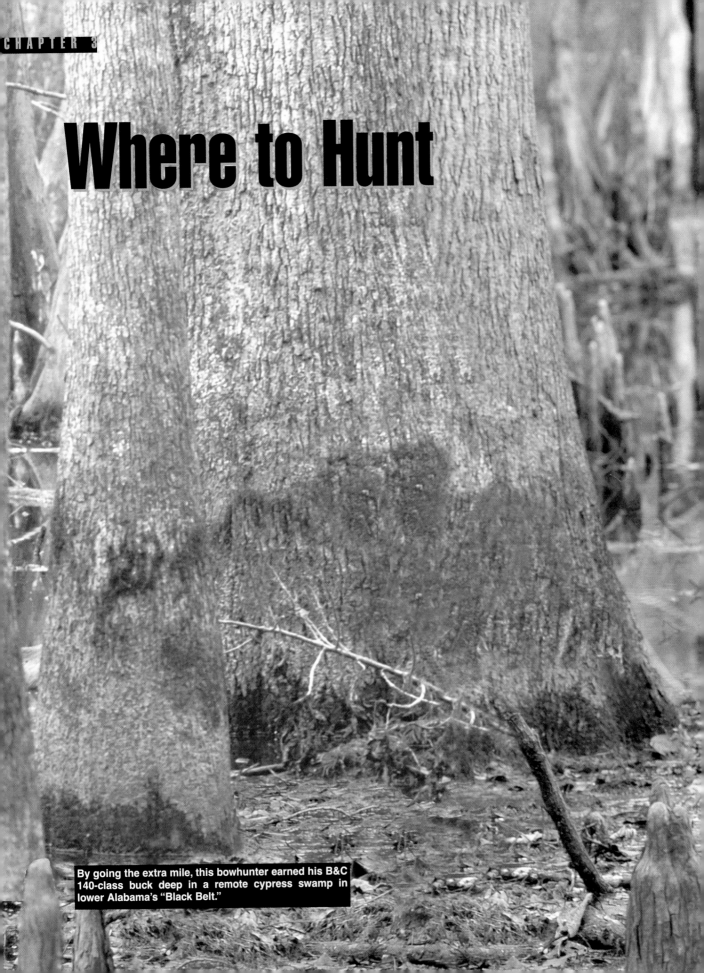

Where to Hunt

By going the extra mile, this bowhunter earned his B&C 140-class buck deep in a remote cypress swamp in lower Alabama's "Black Belt."

East

We all have deer hunts we would like to take. Many whitetail hunters dream of going to areas where the chances of taking a buck of a lifetime are good. Others want to go where they can fill up the freezer with tasty venison. Still others want to go on that special bow- or muzzle-loading hunt or where you can try to bag a buck with your shotgun. I fit in all categories and have devoted the last three decades traveling to areas of special interest to hunt whitetails. Here are some of the shortcuts I have found to finding the hunt you want in the East.

WHERE THE RECORD BOOK BUCKS COME FROM

I don't think I have ever met a white-tailed deer hunter that didn't have a dream hunt for a wall hanger in mind. He may not have had a specific area in mind but he wanted the opportunity to go somewhere where the chances were good of killing a buck larger than any he had taken in the past. If this is the case, then he needs to consider the areas that have a history of producing trophy bucks.

The best way to identify those areas is to study the record books of the Boone & Crockett Club and the Pope & Young Club. The most recent edition of each

of these record books can be purchased from the organizations. (The contact information is listed in the Appendix of this book.) Not only do these record books list the location of where each of these whitetails were taken but in what year, and this is most valuable information. You may not want to plan a hunt to an area that had five record book bucks taken in the 1930s and few since. You want up-to-date information.

A more dramatic way of looking at where these bucks came from is to order the poster-size map of the United States entitled "Boone & Crockett and Pope & Young Record Book White-Tailed Deer: 1991 – 2000" from the Quality Deer Management Association. (Contact information is given in the Appendix of this book.) This map shows, by county, the number of record book deer recorded by both these organizations. It is color shaded by counties and the counties that have produced the highest number of record book class bucks jumps out at you. Since these were the entries for the past decade, it gives you some recent historical data to work with.

If your state, like my state, doesn't have many counties with entries into the record books, you have several other ways of finding the areas where the big bucks are coming from. Contact your Department of Natural Resources and request a report on where the largest bucks in your state are being taken. The type of report you get will vary from state to state. Some states require all deer taken to be checked in at a state run checking station. These records, kept on a computer, can give you current, accurate data. Other states may only have this information for state-run public hunting areas. In either case, they can get you started in the right direction.

READ REPORTS ON BIG BUCKS

Sometimes just reading hunting reports in newspapers and magazines can give you a good idea of where to hunt. One of the best hunts I was ever on in Kentucky came about when, while in Kentucky on business, I read about several large bucks being taken on a public management area in the western part of the state. On a whim, I looked up the county in which the area was located and called the county agent of that county. I told him I would like to hunt on private land that was adjacent to the public hunting area. He told me he didn't know if he could recommend a farmer or not but to give him a day or two and he would see what he could do. The next morning he called me and told me he had a farmer who would like to have a couple of hunters come to his farm and help thin out the bucks that were eating up his soybean crop. I dropped what I was doing and took off to Kentucky.

The next day I spent scouting the farm, especially the part that lay next to the public hunting area. The farmer wasn't a hunter but he was a lot of help with my scouting, as he knew where the bucks were coming off the public area to feed on his crops.

At sunrise the next morning I was sitting where I could watch a well-used deer trail that ran out of the public area. The winding trail ran along the edge of a young pine plantation and into a fence corner that was just a jump away from a soybean field and a temporary pasture. I spent the day there and saw a dozen deer including four young bucks. The second day was about the same. On the third day, the wind caused me to change my stand location. I took an afternoon stand in the young pines where I could see the trail and the fence corner. It would be tight shooting.

About four o'clock in the afternoon, I was half asleep when I was shaken to my senses by a loud rattling sound. There just inside the pines a few yards from me was a huge ten-pointer shoving a smaller six-pointer around. They never knew I was there. It was impossible for me to move, as I was concerned they would see me. They were bumping into pine trees and I had some concern that the fight would wind up in my lap.

Finally, the big buck got the best of the smaller buck and they went back to the trail with the small buck running off. The large buck moved off in the direction of the fence corner. I lost sight of him when some pines came between us. I got my rifle up and got ready for the shot. I could already see the huge buck on my office wall. I waited and waited but he never appeared at the corner. He just disappeared. It was my last day to hunt and while I came home empty-handed, I had a great hunt and all thanks to reading a report from the public hunting area.

Some states have organizations that have big buck contests and/or keep state record books on big bucks, and these organizations can supply you with valuable information as to where in your state the dream bucks are being taken.

HUNTING WHERE DEER ARE PLENTIFUL

Not everyone is trophy hunting and a trophy is a different thing to different people. When I was a teenager I was hooked on deer hunting as much as a boy can be. While there were few deer where I lived I was fortunate enough to have made friends with a deer-hunting expert, the late Ray Householder. Ray studied deer harvest reports from several different states and each fall would go to hot spots he had identified.

One fall, Ray announced to me that he thought it was time for me to go with him on one of his deer hunts. While Ray had taken some trophy bucks he knew I had seen few deer in the wild and just wanted to take my first buck. He picked the Black Warrior Wildlife Management Area near where we lived and planned a camping hunt, with him guiding me. He knew I couldn't afford a hunt far from home and he was wise enough to know I had a lot to learn. I was as excited as a dog with two tails. It was my first big game hunt away from home!

On the third morning of the hunt, the day broke clear and bitterly cold. Back in those days all I had for cold-weather hunting clothes was army surplus clothing, and it certainly wasn't arctic gear by any stretch of the imagination. Ray and I had taken a stand watching a well-used deer trail that was far from the nearest road and ran along a creek bottom.

Midmorning Ray could see that I was near frozen and probably couldn't shoot if a buck showed up with the does we had been seeing all morning. "I know of a large rock overhang near here," he whispered to me, "Why don't we go there and build a fire?"

I hated to admit it but it sounded like a great idea to me.

Soon I was warming by a fire under the cave-like overhang. Adjacent to the overhang was a small waterfall. To me it was like a scene out of a mountain man movie.

As Ray handed me a sandwich he suddenly stopped and whispered "LOOK." There coming down a steep ridge some 100 yards in front of the overhang was a doe walking directly toward us. Just behind her was

This map plots trophy whitetails recorded between 1991 and 2000 in the Boone and Crockett and Pope and Young record books by state and county. To obtain a detailed U.S.G.S. topographical map of your hunting area, log on to:
http://stoegerbooks.mapcard.com.

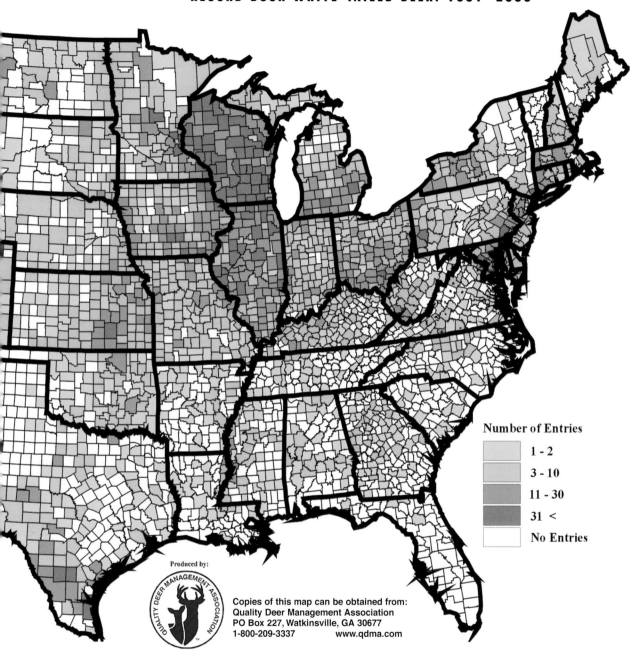

Number of Entries

- 1 - 2
- 3 - 10
- 11 - 30
- 31 <
- No Entries

Produced by:

QUALITY DEER MANAGEMENT ASSOCIATION

Copies of this map can be obtained from:
Quality Deer Management Association
PO Box 227, Watkinsville, GA 30677
1-800-209-3337   www.qdma.com

a spike buck. "Take him!" Ray instructed. I dropped my sandwich, grabbed my old military surplus 1903 Springfield rifle and took aim. At the shot the buck whirled and started back up the ridge. Not waiting, I shot a second time.

The buck went down, hit both times. His little spikes were not much over 4 inches long but I was the most proud hunter that ever hit the woods. At that moment he was the largest buck in the world, a real trophy to me. To this day that is one of the most memo-

rable deer hunts I have ever been on. I have lots of 150+ bucks on my walls but that little spike has a place of honor on my office wall. It is still a trophy.

Hunting where there are lots of deer and where the chances to put venison in the freezer, or to take

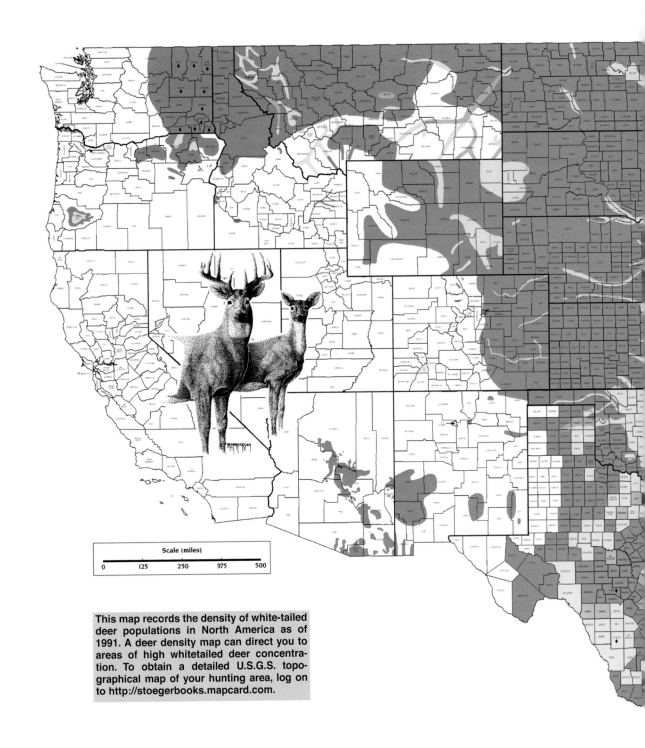

This map records the density of white-tailed deer populations in North America as of 1991. A deer density map can direct you to areas of high whitetailed deer concentration. To obtain a detailed U.S.G.S. topographical map of your hunting area, log on to http://stoegerbooks.mapcard.com.

Scale (miles)
0   125   250   375   500

that first buck is high, has never been easier. The Quality Deer Management Association has a white-tailed deer density map on their website (www.qdma.com) that covers every county in the nation. Also, they sell a poster-size map of the same information that makes it easy to see the deer densities of the counties you may want to consider hunting. Needless to say the higher the deer density the greater the odds for taking deer, provided the weather and other factors cooperate. Also, I should point out that after does have been hunted a few days, they catch on as to what's

WHITE-TAILED DEER DENSITY MAP

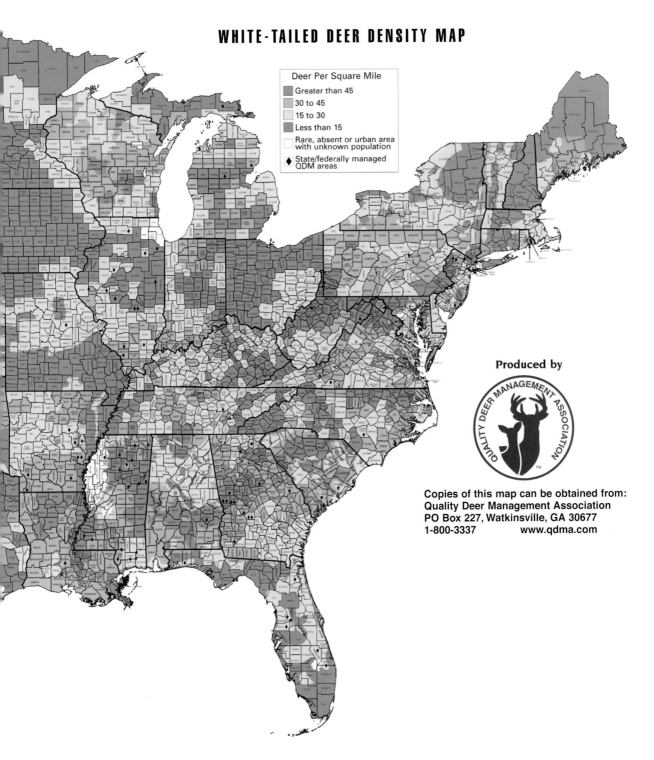

Deer Per Square Mile

■ Greater than 45
■ 30 to 45
■ 15 to 30
■ Less than 15
□ Rare, absent or urban area with unknown population
◆ State/federally managed QDM areas

Produced by

QUALITY DEER MANAGEMENT ASSOCIATION

Copies of this map can be obtained from:
Quality Deer Management Association
PO Box 227, Watkinsville, GA 30677
1-800-3337   **www.qdma.com**

going on and can become just as difficult as bucks to find. Some of the most fun and challenging hunts I have been on have been doe hunts.

Most state game and fish agencies can give you the counties and wildlife management areas in the state that has high deer populations. Usually hunters are encouraged to hunt there to keep the deer numbers in check.

In states where there is a deer management assistance program, private landowners are given doe permits and many times large landowners would appreciate responsible hunters helping har-

Special hunts limited to muzzleloaders (above) or shot-guns offer great opportunities for hunting whitetails.

vest the does. These farms are a great place to start a new deer hunter on his hunting career. Not only are the odds good for success, but they learn that the hunter is a part of the wildlife management program by taking animals that take the local deer population over the carrying capacity of the land. It is a lesson in the wise use of wildlife resources.

FINDING SPECIAL HUNTS

Some of the best hunts for trophy-class bucks and for does are on special use areas such as military bases, university lands, and other large tracts of land where hunting is not normally conducted. These hunts are often in areas where, due to other human activities and safety concerns, the hunts are restricted to bows, muzzleloading rifles, or shotguns. A growing number of towns are finding hunting as a means of controlling swelling whitetail populations.

Many of these special hunts are not promoted outside the local area and you must spend some time researching them to find them.

One fall, I heard about a deer hunt on some university-owned land that had a reputation for producing good scoring bucks. I started calling the university and it took me a number of calls to finally get the right person, someone who knew "what in the world I was talking about." They were indeed holding a hunt and I managed to get a permit for the two-day hunt.

The first morning of the hunt, soon after daylight, I found an old logging road that had a number of fresh scrapes in it. I looked no farther and took a seat at the base of a large beech tree where I could see the scrapes. No sooner had I gotten settled in, a 148 B&C buck came up the road and started working the first scrape he came to. One shot later my hunt was over. The unknown hunt had been a winner.

Contact the public affairs officer at military bases, large landowning universities, and any other land base operation where you think the hunting would be good. All they can do is say no and who knows they may be planning a hunt.

I have been fortunate enough to hunt most of the eastern states for deer and know firsthand that there are areas in every state where the prospects for finding big bucks are good. Also there are areas in every state where chances for getting a deer for the freezer are good. It takes a little research to find the best spots and a little luck, plus skill, to fill the tag but it can be done. The search for new and better places to hunt is part of the hunt and extends the hunt into the nonhunting months.

West

Do you remember your first trophy whitetail buck? I do! It was the first buck I ever shot. I took it with my maternal grandfather's single-shot 12-gauge shotgun. Size of his antlers, number of points? Does it really matter? It didn't to me. But in case you're wondering, that spike was and still is the "best" buck I have ever taken. In so saying, please realize I have since taken a considerable number of much bigger bucks, including several which gross score in excess of 170 Boone & Crockett points. But to me that little spike, whose neck mount now hangs on my office wall was and remains every bit as an important a "trophy" as the 187 B&C point buck that hangs beside it.

To me a "trophy" is a remembrance of a great hunt, special friends and occasions. Thus, trophy bucks can be found throughout the whitetail's range in the East or in the West.

MATURE BUCKS

Several years ago I made the decision to hunt primarily for mature bucks, those being four years old or older. This, shortly after I realized I had killed a year-old buck that could have grown up to become a record book contender. I wished dearly I could have breathed life back into that buck. Since that time I have remained true to my promise. The only times I have strayed is when hunting in areas where there are virtually no mature deer. In those areas I've simply hunted for a representative buck of the region. And in most times, when hunting where few if any mature bucks exist I leave camp without taking a buck, quite often instead having taken a doe.

There are some basics to consider when you decide to become a "trophy hunter"; in this instance meaning hunting for bucks with antlers bigger than most other deer in the area. Deciding to do so generally cuts down the odds of taking a deer, you may go home empty-handed.

If you plan on hunting for "trophy" deer with the reasonable expectation of taking such a buck, you have to hunt where they exist in reasonable numbers.

Whitetail bucks tend to start producing their best antlers at four years of age and continue producing their better antlers through age seven or eight, if they receive adequate nutrition. Once their body and skeletal systems are fully developed, any nutrients not required for body maintenance can be channeled into antler development. Not all bucks that reach maturity develop huge antlers. Many simply develop into nice eight- to ten-point bucks with medium mass and decent tine lengths, but still most are the kind many deer hunters would be tickled taking. Truly monstrously antlered bucks are practically freaks of nature. Although in recent years it seems the average rack size of whitetails is increasing, thanks primarily to improved nutritional levels and allowing bucks to get a bit older before hunting pressure is placed on them. Throughout the continent there seems to be more and more emphasis these days placed on quality buck and quality deer management, resulting in larger antlers and body sizes.

THE WEST'S BIGGEST BUCKS

Tony Knight used a .50 caliber Knight MK-85 muzzleloader to drop this 178 B&C buck in western Iowa, one of his favorite hot spots for large bucks.

Where do you find the biggest bucks? Big bucks occur where they have the opportunity to mature in the presence of good, daily nutrition. They occur basically in two different situations; where the deer herd is intensively managed (as they are in a great portion of Texas) and where food is plentiful and hunting pressure is light. These two situations occur throughout much of the western portion of the continent.

Yet there are also hotspots for trophy deer, areas which in the past have produced numerous Boone & Crockett Record Book entries. And with whitetails there is no reason to believe these same areas will not continue to produce record book bucks, as long as the hunting pressure does not drastically increase or the deer populations are allowed to increase beyond the range's carrying capacity for an extended period of time. Notably those areas include portions of southern and northern Texas, portions of the states of Oklahoma, Kansas, Nebraska, both North and South Dakota, eastern Colorado, eastern Wyoming, Montana and Idaho, and the Canadian Provinces of Alberta, Saskatchewan, Manitoba, as well as portions of British Columbia.

All these areas have produced record book bucks and many average-size mature deer for the areas (which by eastern standards would be huge in body and antler).

Some hot spots for big whitetails come and go because once the word gets out many hunters desire to hunt those areas. In several of the western states this situation is a bit different than elsewhere because the best whitetail hunting occurs on private lands where managers limit the take of deer, or the state's wildlife department issues only so many licenses for particular areas through a lottery drawing. Such is the case in western Iowa where I have frequently hunted and Kansas where I wish I could hunt more often. Nonresident deer hunting is closely regulated in these areas by the number of deer tags issued in specific management units.

Given an open-ended opportunity to hunt for the biggest deer, I would opt for hunting in Kansas and Iowa. These two particular states seem to have the gene pool, nutrition, and an abundance of mature bucks necessary to produce extremely large antlered bucks. There is no doubt that any given year there are at least one or more bucks in each of these states that could be a new world record whitetail! The same can probably be said of the Canadian Provinces of Alberta and Saskatchewan.

The biggest typical whitetail buck I have ever seen appeared almost 12 o'clock noon just a few miles south of Athabaska, Alberta. He was chasing a doe on the side of the road. The buck had 10 extremely long points. Main beams that would easily have exceeded 30 inches in length and as massive a rack as I have ever seen. His outside spread approached 30 inches. There is no doubt in my mind he would have easily gross scored in the

220 B&C range and netted mightily close to the same.

I watched him for about 90 seconds and got every look at him I wanted except for me standing over him right after I shot him. Alas, he was safe, on property in our unit but on land we did not have permission to hunt. His sight is one I will never, ever forget!

Such bucks exist throughout several western whitetail areas. They have been there for years and will continue to be in those same areas for years to come.

I mentioned Iowa earlier as one of my top choices for monstrous bucks. I've hunted western Iowa several times, thanks to drawing a late muzzleloader season tag through their lottery drawing system. The last afternoon of my first hunt, with moments remaining before the season closed at sundown, I shot an extremely old and impressive buck we had seen earlier in the hunt. Chances are you too have seen him if you watched the opening sequences of the "Bass Pro's Outdoor World" television show. It's the buck seen running through the snow.

I shot the buck while still hunting in knee-deep snow while a blustery wind dropped the chill factor to about 20 below zero. The locals called him "The Mule Deer" because they thought him too wide to be

Abundant hot spots in the western United States and Canada can yield Boone & Crockett record book bucks.

This monster ten-pointer was taken near Athabaska in Alberta, Canada.

a whitetail. Back at camp that night we measured his spread at just short of 28 inches. His main beams were 30 and 31 inches in length, the longest main beams on any buck I have taken. His bases easily measured 6 inches. A basic eight-pointer with one split brow tine and about a 2-inch drop-tine on the other side, he gross scored about 178 B&C points. He was truly a trophy deer, but not just because of his big antlers. I hunted the buck throughout most of the late muzzleloader season during blizzard and near blizzard conditions, and finally took him during the waning moments of the season.

Another buck I shot in Iowa was taken during the regular shotgun season (again having drawn a whitetail tag through the lottery drawing). Although a shotgun season, I used a .50 caliber Knight MK-85 muzzleloader just as with the other buck, while also attending the Iowa Governor's Whitetail Hunt.

The evening before I arrived in Iowa I hunted an Indian Reservation in Saskatchewan. There, just before dark I shot an extremely nice basic ten-pointer with a couple of "kickers," using a .300 Win Mag Remington Model 700. That buck gross scored about 165 B&C. Shortly after taking care of the meat, cape, and antlers I boarded a plane to Iowa.

The following afternoon I was sitting in a ground blind on the edge of a field I had previously hunted. Steve Shoop of J&S Trophy Hunts had selected the location. During a blowing snowstorm with about

10 minutes of legal shooting time (till sundown) remaining I spotted a sizable buck behind me. He had a big neck, floppy skin about his face and brisket, and pot-bellied appearance. His antlers looked big, even when compared to his body, which I was certain would field-dress in excess of 220 pounds.

When he turned slightly and presented a better angle at his vitals I pulled the trigger. Moments later I picked up a broad blood trail in the rapidly falling snow. Within less than 30 yards I found my buck. He had 14 total points, a typical twelve-pointer with double brow tines on each side. Later he scored 174 B&C points. Interestingly that same week campmates took three other bucks that gross-scored above 170 points. Jerry Martin, fellow member of the RedHead Pro Hunting Team, unsuccessfully stalked a huge typical twelve-pointer that would likely have scored in the 180s. Unfortunately the buck left the area before Jerry could get a shot.

Do I like Iowa? You better believe it!

Kansas, I have not hunted as often as I want or hope to in the future.

I do have several friends and acquaintances that have been extremely fortunate in drawing limited Kansas licenses or they were able to procure landowner tags. The bucks they have taken are simply monstrous. Even the average bucks they have taken are bigger than most hunters will ever have a reasonable chance of taking. The southwestern corner seems to be a hot spot at present for big whitetails, but big whitetails exist throughout the state. I am reluctant to mention specific units in Kansas, just as in Iowa because by the time you read this the best units to apply for may well change.

One of the other western hot spots that has long been a leader in producing good and monstrous antlered deer is Texas. Big deer in terms of antlers exist on ranches throughout Texas, especially in South Texas where deer herds are intensively managed. I have hunted whitetails throughout North America including some of the famous hunting preserves. Outside of a few such operations as the Sanctuary in Michigan, Timberghost in Iowa, and Heartland Ranches in Missouri most whitetail hunting areas pale when compared to hunting a good Texas ranch. I know of no other place where on a good day you can see 20 to 40 or more bucks and at least half would be considered "shooters" anywhere.

One year I hunted on Tim Schmidt's Double D Ranches, actually a bit north of the famed South Texas Brush Country. In a single afternoon I rattled up 42 bucks including some absolute monsters. It was on that same ranch I shot my widest whitetail ever, a buck with 12 points and a nearly 29-inch outside spread.

Hunting Texas for whitetails has become an expensive proposition, especially when hunting some of the better ranches. Even though hunting there is expensive there are few if any whitetail destinations which can compare to what you'll see and experience on a well-managed Texas whitetail ranch.

Eastern Colorado is another hot spot for big whitetails. Hunting there is by drawing or procuring a landowner tag. In the better whitetail habitat in

this area it is also quite common to encounter big mule deer. On a recent hunt a good friend and hunting partner, Richard Petrini, owner of Tri-State Outfitting, guided a client to a record book mule deer in the morning and another client to a record book whitetail that afternoon.

One of my best eight-pointers ever, — net scored as a six-pointer because of one missing brow tine — scored in excess of 160 B&C points. I shot him on the edge of an alfalfa field next to a small creek bottom while hunting with Petrini in eastern Colorado.

For several years I hunted in the Canadian Provinces of Alberta and Saskatchewan. As mentioned earlier I saw the biggest whitetail I have ever seen in Alberta. But seeing and taking are two different things. I have seen some extremely good deer in Alberta, but I have never taken a truly big deer there. I have, however, taken several mature, really nice bucks that score in the high 140s. The same is true for Saskatchewan. I missed one of the three Boone & Crockett whitetails I have had a chance at in Saskatchewan. My best buck came from the Ochap Indian Reservation, the one I described having taken right before heading to Iowa.

Country music star John Anderson nailed this 160-Class B & C buck during a frigid hunt in southeastern Iowa.

When to Hunt

A snow-covered wall tent pitched in an icy forest supports Wayne Fears' motto: "The best time to go deer hunting is every opportunity you get."

East

A neighbor of mine recently asked me to come over to his house to discuss his deer hunting program. He had a job that involved a lot of travel, so he couldn't pick the times he could go deer hunting. It seemed that every chance he had to hunt, the weather was either too warm, too windy, or raining. Or there was a full moon.

Over a cup of coffee we discussed how he hunted each of these and many other situations, and I quickly learned that he was staying home during many of these "bad days" when he should have been out hunting. He was not matching hunting techniques with the changes he was facing.

WEATHER CHANGES

While I am an advocate of the premise that the best time to go hunting is every opportunity you get, regardless of the weather, there are certain weather changes that every hunter should be aware of. Any time that a front is coming into an area, deer tend to feed up heavily before the front arrives. In managing deer at hunting lodges, I have seen deer feed heavily as much as 36 hours before a major frontal system pushes through. Then the deer will lay up as the frontal system, and all the rain or snow that's associated with it, pushes through. Immediately behind the front, there is usually cold weather with clear skies, and again, deer will be moving. Hunters who can pick their times to hunt based on the weather would do well to take advantage of the 24 to 36 hours before a major front comes through and immediately following the passage of a front when the weather turns cold and clear. Techniques that work during these times are many and varied. Watching a good feeding area as the deer feed up before and after the front and trail watching are generally good during this type of weather.

One of my favorite times to stalk hunt is in association with the passage of frontal systems. This is especially true if I want to hunt all day long. As the front approaches, deer are not selective of the period of time they feed. I have seen extremely heavy feeding activity in the middle of the day just prior to a front reaching an area. This, in my opinion, makes one of the most ideal situations for the stalk hunter. If you can't pick your times to hunt or just want to take advantage of every opportunity, hunt during the rainy weather but change your methods accordingly.

It was one of the wettest mornings I had ever seen in a lifetime of deer hunting. A cold front was moving in and the day broke in a steady downpour of rain and a bone-chilling temperature of 40 degrees.

I had spent the morning stalk hunting a hardwood-covered ridge where I had been seeing plenty of deer. On this wet morning I saw no deer and was as wet and cold as I had ever been. By eleven o'clock I had about all I could take and started down a logging road that led to the field where I had left my truck parked.

Having walked most of the distance to the field I came upon two other soggy hunters who had also spent the morning in this miserable weather without so much as seeing one whitetail. As we discussed our lack of sanity for hunting on such a wet, cold day, I saw a flicker of movement under some cedars off to my right some 75 yards away. As our conversation continued, I studied the lines under the low-growing trees and suddenly I made out three heads. Two were does with their necks stretched up and their eyes glued on us. Behind them under a separate cedar I could make out a buck, his head held low to the ground with his antlers laid back. All three deer were bedded down under the thick growing eastern red cedars where little moisture could penetrate. They were convinced we could not see them and were holding tight.

I said nothing to the two other hunters about what I was seeing. As soon as they walked off, I eased around to a slight ridge in order to get a shot at the buck. As I eased up to a large oak and started shouldering my rifle, the does decided I had spotted them and got up running. I never saw where or how the buck left. He just seemed to disappear.

That afternoon, after a hot lunch and a change into dry clothing. I once again went back into the cold rain to hunt. This time I carried a pair of Swarovski binoculars and started working on a new hunting technique. I looked for areas that looked as though they would offer deer some protection from the constant cold rain. When I found an area such as low-growing cedars or other evergreens, I stopped and spent several minutes spotting every square inch with my binoculars. I did the same thing in thick blown-down treetops.

By three o'clock, I was amazed at how many deer I had found bedded down. One nice buck went home with me as proof that my newfound fowl-weather technique, although requiring a lot of looking and patience, did work.

A lot of hunters tend to sit in the camp or stay at home during a period of several days of hard rain. However, those hunters who are willing to put together a small man drive will often find this an ideal time to conduct drives. The deer are hesitant to get up, and when they do get up, they move slowly, trying to slip through the wet woods and it gives the alert stander an opportunity to get a shot at a buck that otherwise he might never see.

On foggy, drizzly days, I have seen bucks get up from the bed to feed for a short period during midday, especially in agricultural fields such as wheat, soybeans, corn, or alfalfa. This is a good time to

Protected by effective foul-weather gear, even a hunt in hard rain can produce a trophy whitetail.

spend the day on a stand overlooking such crops. It is also a good time to stalk hunt, as you can move about very quietly. The secret is to use the drive technique if it is a hard rain and to sit on a stand or stalk if it is a drizzle.

UNUSUALLY WARM WEATHER

In many eastern states, the hunting season opens while the weather is still warm. This is especially true when bowhunting. In some states, there are sudden warm spells when the weather should be cold. Often when hunting during warm weather, the hunter finds that the deer movement during the day comes to a virtual standstill. It causes two changes in deer behavior, especially among bucks. The first change is that bucks will tend to feed most heavily at night when it is much cooler. Secondly, bucks tend to spend the daylight hours held up in thick cover such as beaver swamps, young planted pines, cane breaks along creeks, in brier patches, and other locations offering shade and protection. My favorite hunting technique for unusually warm weather is to put a portable tree stand high in a tree overlooking a creek or beaver swamp. I get into the stand by midafternoon and stay alert until dark. Often deer activity will pick up at last light. I depend upon a good binocular and a quality riflescope with at least a 40mm objective lens for hunting during these low light conditions.

A stand in a feeding area can be good during this warm weather if you will study the edge of the forest around the food plot or field at dusk with your binoculars. Many times, I have seen bucks stand back in the woods waiting for dark on a warm evening before they venture into the opening to feed.

In the Deep South and even in swampy areas of the North, it is necessary to take insect repellent with you to the stand to avoid spending the afternoon swatting mosquitoes.

MOON PHASES

There is a tremendous amount of discussion these days about the affect the moon has on deer feeding. The one thing I feel sure of, based on my own observations while managing whitetail deer, is that deer are going to feed on bright nights, such as when the moon is full. During these bright nights, I prefer to hunt late in the afternoon, as it has been my experience that deer will feed from late afternoon until late in the night, and then bed down until late afternoon the following day. So during the bright phases of the moon, I wait until three or four o'clock in the afternoon to go hunting, then I try to locate a stand where I am observing deer moving from their bedding areas to the feeding areas. Many times it has been a productive method of hunting.

FOOD AVAILABILITY

The change in available food for deer is significant in that it may determine where and how we hunt. Deer are opportunists when it comes to feeding. During the early part of the deer season or during years when there is very heavy mast production, deer can be found feeding in red oak and white oak groves. The alert hunter can take advantage of this by setting up his stand overlooking an area offering abundant food. However, I feel that a better opportunity for a deer

Bucks may become nocturnal during periods of bright moonlight, and prefer to bed down in the shadows during daylight hours

hunter is during those years when mast production is low or almost nonexistent. Then deer are forced to look for a second choice of food, and usually, in most of the whitetail range, this is low-growing vines, such as greenbrier or Japanese honeysuckle. The hunter who has done his scouting and located food of this type will do well to place a stand overlooking this food source.

During periods of low mast production, deer also tend to move into agricultural areas, such as soybeans, wheat, corn, or whatever is available that they can eat. During falls when there was absolutely no mast production, I have seen deer break their traditional early morning and late afternoon feeding habits and feed in agricultural fields during all hours of the day. This is especially true in standing corn.

The wise hunter will scout his area thoroughly and observe the changes that are occurring in the availability of food. Hunt where the deer's food is located, and that's where you will find the deer. A lack of acorns is no reason to stay home or think that the hunting is going to be poor. A good greenbrier patch, cornfield, or honeysuckle thicket may produce more bucks in a concentrated area than you have ever seen underneath the big white oak tree.

HUNTING PRESSURE

Hunting pressure makes a tremendous change in deer movement. While deer don't think as we think, they do get conditioned to the movements of man and respond accordingly. If I am going to hunt in an area that has had a lot of hunting pressure for two or three weeks, I will sleep late, eat a leisurely breakfast, and get out on my hunt at about 9 a.m. I hunt hard from nine until about two o'clock, then I retire back to camp for an afternoon of fishing or perhaps scouting. Large bucks catch on quickly to the fact that most hunting is done early in the morning at daybreak and late in the afternoon at sunset. Since most hunters tend to return to camp or to their cars or go back to work at eight or nine o'clock in the morning, the woods are generally quiet with only a few hunters around at midday. This is the time that big bucks pick to move.

The hunter who enjoys having the woods almost to himself can either set up a stand or stalk hunt in areas of heavy hunting pressure during the midday hours, and while they may not see as many young bucks and does, if they do see a deer, chances are it will be a good, heavy-racked buck.

Hunting pressure also greatly affects the area that I select to hunt. Heavy hunting pressure generally occurs around areas easy for hunters to get to, such as roads, food plots, agricultural fields, and other places of this type. The hunter going into an area that has received heavy hunting pressure should study a map carefully. Select the overlooked areas that are more difficult to get to and hunt in there.

You will be surprised at the number of deer that have retreated from the areas of heavy pressure to the underhunted spots. In here, they are relaxed and going about their normal routine. Often around my hunting lodges I have seen nice bucks moving in areas that are never hunted, such as near the lodge, close to the rifle range, or property that requires wading a creek or swamp to get to. Here the deer are not reacting so much to the pressure and are relatively easy to hunt, compared to those deer that are along roads, food plots, etc., where hunting pressure is heavy day in and day out.

DOG PRESSURE

Hunters often complain of having problems finding deer in areas that are thought to have high populations of deer. Upon further investigation, they frequently find that feral or freely ranging dogs are running heavily day in and day out. Under these conditions, deer tend to bed down and move more at night. In fact, I have seen areas where deer were almost totally nocturnal because of a heavy free-range dog population. In such a situation, hunters would be wise to consider small man drives or still hunting in areas that are difficult for dogs to get to, such as islands in the middle of a beaver swamp or small, isolated areas, such as thick swamps along a creek bottom.

Heavy pressure by dogs can do much to upset the opportunity for hunters, even where there is a high deer population. So when scouting, be on the lookout for signs of heavy dog usage, especially in a deer hunting tract that is surrounded by small farms, tenant houses, or other places where people have a lot of yard dogs. This situation is often one of the most complicated to work out a hunting system that works.

THE RUT

Needless to say, the rut makes major changes in the movement of bucks in the woods. The main thing to keep in mind is that during the rut, bucks have thrown caution to the wind and are liable to be seen at any time of the day or night.

Learn to locate active scrapes and go prepared to watch these scrapes all day for as many as three consecutive days. In areas where there is a low buck-doe ratio, rattling should be considered. There is no question that the changes that occur during the rut provide excellent hunting opportunities, and the hunter whose season allows him to hunt during the rut should take advantage of this time. These are some of the major changes that occur in the woods during the deer season. By studying these changes and changing your tactics appropriately, you can make each one of them work for you to help you become a more successful deer hunter.

After I reviewed these changes with my neighbor, he was amazed at how many of these situations were occurring where he hunted and how he had failed to take advantage of the changes. Hunting deer should never be constant; always be ready to change tactics as situations dictate change. By doing so, you will have more venison on your table each year.

Wayne Fears busted this mature whitetail at midday, a time when hunting pressure is usually low.

West

When should you hunt whitetails? If there is a whitetail season going on and you have a license for that particular season, GO HUNTING! Don't look for excuses not to go hunting or to be unsuccessful in the field while pursuing whitetails. Only writers kill a lot of big whitetails while sitting in front of a computer or word processor, everyone else has to do it in the field.

Before getting into my personal observations about the effects of weather, moon phases, hunting pressure, special seasons and ideal times to be in the field, let me remind you whitetailed deer are individuals. Like you and me, deer have our their way of doing things. Sometimes what and how we do things may coincide with how others do things, and we follow the crowd. But other times we do things contra to what anyone else does.

I love being in the field when weather conditions are at their worst. Not a whole lot of other hunters like being out then, but I do because I generally have the hunting area to myself. Whitetails and especially mature bucks are no different in how they do things. There are always exceptions to any "rule."

We as hunters and readers about hunting whitetails, as well as viewers of videos and television hunting shows, have our personal heroes. One of mine

happens to be the co-author of this book. J. Wayne Fears is someone who not only knows how to talk the talk he has walked the walk, so to speak. Wayne Fears knows deer and deer hunting. He's spent a lifetime not only studying whitetails, managing their herds and habitat, but has hunted extensively with every legal means that can be used to hunt whitetails and has done so throughout North America. His observations are based on personal experiences and research he's done and that which was done by those for whom he has respect.

We all need heroes. Choose mentors and heroes who know whereof they speak, tempered with many years of hands-on experience. Just because you have read it in a magazine or for that matter seen it on a video or television show, doesn't necessarily mean that's exactly the way things happen. There are always exceptions and sometimes it's the biggest antlered mature bucks that are the exception.

What follows are my observations based on 50 years (as this is being written) of whitetail hunting experience, and 30 plus years of experiences as a wildlife biologist and researcher who specialized in whitetails.

If there's one thing I've learned during my years of hunting and working as a biologist it is that there is still more to learn about whitetails than I have learned up to this point. Whitetails are a dynamic species, ever-changing and adapting.

EFFECTS OF WEATHER ON DEER

Deer can "feel" changes in barometric pressure. They can sense the approach of storm systems. But they can neither determine the length nor the severity of the storms.

During the late fall and early winter as frontal systems approach it has been my experience that deer tend to feed before the cold fronts arrive. Thus, I plan to be in the field the day or two immediately before frontal passage, if my schedule allows me to do so.

During the worst part of the storm most deer tend to lay low until the worst has passed. But that is not always the case with every deer. One of the nicer Canadian deer and my two biggest bucks from Iowa were taken when the snow was blown horizontally during blizzard-like conditions. Undoubtedly those bucks failed to read the rule books.

TEMPERATURE EXTREMES

Cold is a relative "term." What's cold for Regina, Saskatchewan, and Laredo, Texas, are entirely different matters. During November deer in Canada and the other northern climes of the West tend to move better when it is extremely cold, especially during the rut. Yet if the temperature drops into the teens in South Texas, chances are excellent you are not going to see a deer until the temperature starts to warm a bit.

It's been my experience that cold temperatures tend to cause deer to move or be very active in some areas and cause them to crawl into a bed and stay there in others.

One of the things to remember, the farther north you go in the realm of the whitetail, the longer and thicker their hair coats. One of the best examples of how cooler weather "works" on deer is to compare them to you or me wearing long underwear, several layers of wool and down, covered with a heavy overcoat so that we're dressed for the coldest of winter weather, because that is how deer are "dressed" going into the late fall. If the temperature becomes extremely cold, we're prepared for it, but may find it more comfortable to move a bit and then rest safely

out of the cold wind. Deer may do the same. Forget for a moment that I've told you I love being out in the severest of weather.

Now conversely let's imagine we are wearing the same winter clothes and the temperatures become comparatively balmy. Wearing all those clothes are you going to be extremely active? I doubt it and I know I'm not. Deer react the same way.

When wearing all our winter clothes, there is a temperature range at which we are fairly comfortable, and thus we are quite active. When the thermometer is within this range, we're going to move around a lot more than at either of the extremes. The same is true for deer.

This is pretty well the case throughout the whitetail's range. But there again are exceptions in terms of individuals and extenuating circumstances such as becoming extremely hungry. We'll wait as long as we can at either of the temperature extremes, but eventually we're going to have to try to find something to eat.

I often hear how cooler weather affects the whitetail's breeding season in a positive manner. It does so simply because of the comfort level. If it turns unusually warm during the local deer herd's breeding season, the does don't quit coming into estrus. The chasing and breeding is usually done after nightfall when the temperatures are cooler.

RAINFALL

Rain affects deer in particular areas quite differently. I've hunted in the East in Alabama and as soon as the rain started, deer activity totally ceased and stayed at a standstill until it quit raining.

In South Texas and northern Mexico rain has the opposite effect, creating a tendency to greatly increase deer activity. An elderly Mexican vaquero explained the phenomenon by simply suggesting "Big bucks like to walk in wet sand!" I've seen pretty much the same thing happen throughout much of the West, with the exception being a couple of hunts I was on in Saskatchewan during an early fall season. It rained quite a bit on those hunts and we saw few deer, but then in all fairness we hardly saw any deer movement that entire week, regardless of whether it was raining or not.

WIND

Wind in some instances can have a dramatic effect on deer, but it's more of a local "thing" rather than a uni-

Standing within a snow-covered deadfall, Larry Weishuhn abides by his own rule: "Don't look for excuses for not going hunting."

versal "thing." A few years ago there was research done which showed: deer activity was high when the wind was blowing less than 15 miles per hour; activity slowed between 15 and 20 miles per hour; and ceased when it blew 20 to 25 miles per hour. This research was done in a portion of Texas where the winds seldom blow beyond about 15 miles per hour.

Over the years I've hunted a lot of different areas including the eastern portion of Wyoming, where the wind never ceased blowing. Here deer are used to winds blowing all of the time. Strong winds, when I have hunted there, did not make western plains deer overly jumpy or nervous. Yet I have been in other areas of the West where the winds tended to make some deer extremely nervous perhaps because of the jerky movement of leaves, or the sounds of wind blowing which interfered with the deer's ability to hear approaching danger, or the wind was "messing with" its sense of smell. For whatever reason, some of the individual deer I watched were extremely nervous. Others confronted with those same wind velocities in the same area seemed to hardly even notice the wind was blowing. Deer are not all cut from the same mold. Me? I believe in going hunting, weather or not!

THE MOON'S EFFECT ON BREEDING SEASONS

In recent years we've seen a tremendous amount written about the effects of the moon on deer activity, including their breeding season. These findings are all very interesting.

In terms of the rut, most whitetail breeding seasons seem to occur so that seven and a half months later the fawns are born for that region's most nutritious time period during the spring or in some instances summer. Interestingly, breeding dates sometimes vary greatly within states or even fairly close geographic areas. In Texas, a state with which I am most familiar, our whitetail breeding seasons vary considerably. In the area I grew up just north of the Texas Gulf Coast, we occasionally saw bucks breeding does in mid- to late September. A few miles

Midday hunting can be effective during various moon phases when dawn and dusk activity is slow or nonexistent.

farther south and east the whitetail rut occurred in late August. A bit north and west the rut occurred the first couple weeks of November, to the south and west the peak of the rut occurred in mid-December. New or old moon did not seem to make much difference, the peak of the rut seldom changes.

Since the 1960s whitetail does from the Brush Country of South Texas have been periodically collected, their fetuses taken and measured crown to rump to determine the peak breeding dates. For the past practically 40 years, the Brush Country's peak breeding date has been December 18.

In northern areas of the West things may be a bit different, but I doubt seriously breeding dates vary more than a week or so either way from one year to the next.

I suspect of greater annual bearing upon breeding dates are the body conditions of the does, as determined by their current nutritional conditions and whether or not they have been nursing twin fawns throughout the summer and early fall.

The decreasing amount of daylight, signaling the coming of winter and the spring which is surely to follow have the greatest bearing of when does breed.

Bucks on the other hand are ready to breed basically during the time they are in "hard antlers." This is a time when great amounts of testosterone courses their veins.

THE MOON'S EFFECT ON DEER ACTIVITY

Quite a few years ago four friends and I decided to maintain a record of each time we saw white-tailed deer, making note of time of day and activity in which the deer were involved. We maintained a year-round record of the deer observed, not just during hunting seasons but also during our travels.

What prompted our interest in moon-based activity charts was the fact that several fishermen such as David O'Keeffe frequently planned their fishing times around "Solunar Tables." These were based to a great extent on moon phases and positioning. O'Keeffe had noticed he saw considerable deer activity on the sides of the lakes and streams he fished during peak suggested fishing times. I had heard the same from other fishermen and often wondered how the "Solunar Tables" related to deer movement.

Initially I set out with one of the activity charts in hand, but then soon decided it would be better to record all deer sightings, time of day and their activity, and then go back and look at the activity charts after the fact.

The five of us kept good records throughout the entire year and part of the next before we graphed what each of us had seen and when. Then we "laid over" the peak activity times for fishing. Amazingly, the observed peak movements and the suggested peak movement periods tracked extremely closely. After that we started paying a lot more attention to the activity charts published in different magazines. While we did not particularly plan our hunts around suggested peak movement periods, we made certain, when possible, that we were in the field when they were supposed to occur.

Jeff Murray and others have since published several activity charts of when to expect peak and minor deer movement periods. These quite often prove to be highly accurate and would likely be even more accurate if we lived in a "Utopian world." Unfortunately we don't!

Factors which can affect this predicted deer movement include food availability, extreme weather conditions (although my friend Gary Roberson of game calling fame tells me with predators, weather has no negative affect when it comes to varmints responding to calls at the times charts suggest activity should be at its peak). Other factors which may affect activity differences include breeding seasons, deer density, and predator density (including human and hunting pressure).

I'm not suggesting you plan your entire hunting schedule around the activity charts. But, I would strongly suggest that if possible that you be in the field when major feeding and activity peaks are to occur, as suggested on these charts.

As a sideline I will say that I particularly hunt during the middle of the day when the moon is full or nearly so the night before, and also when there is virtually no moon the night before. I've seen excellent activity by mature bucks during the middle of the day under both those "moon" conditions.

HUNTING PRESSURE

Hunting pressure means different things in different areas. When I was growing up, after our deer herds started increasing, if you did not shoot a deer during the first week of the season your chances of taking a deer that year were greatly reduced. This was partly because a tremendous number of bucks were taken opening day and few remained, and those that did became extremely wary.

These days hunting pressure in the West is not as big a deal as it is in the East. This, because the number of hunters on any given property is usually considerably less in the West than what you would find on the same-size property in the East. On many western properties the numbers of deer taken are closely regulated and what hunting pressure there is, is often spread out over the length of the season. I

realize there are exceptions.

What to do when considering hunting where hunter pressure is heavy, if I'm looking for a particularly large antlered deer? To be honest, I'll hunt somewhere else where there is less hunting pressure and bucks have an opportunity to mature before being taken.

But, if I have little choice in the matter I'll plan my hunting strategies around how competing hunters hunt. If they are walkers, I'll try to position myself where there is a good chance the others might push deer to me. If they hunt only early and late, I'll stay out all day long. Whether a natural phenomenon or something we have taught deer, big bucks often move during the middle of the day when most hunters are back at camp watching television or fortifying their own bodies with food. If there is any movement during the middle of the day, I want to be in the field when it occurs.

Hunting where there is considerable pressure? I'll also look for places to go where others are not hunting. Perhaps that means hunting close to camp, or close to a major highway, or even a grassy field everyone has previously avoided. Look for places to hunt that others don't.

A few years ago I shot a particularly nice multi-tined buck in Wyoming a relatively short distance from a major highway, this in an area other hunters in that camp did not want to hunt because of occasional "road noise." Another time in South Texas, I arrived after other hunters had headed out for the afternoon and I was uncertain as to where they might be. So I sat down less than 50 yards from camp where I could watch a narrow "sendero" leading to a water hole. Less than 30 minutes later, I put my tag on an extremely long-tined eight-pointer with a couple of "kickers." It turned out to be the biggest buck taken that hunt.

SPECIAL SEASONS

Special seasons can be a tremendous help in taking big whitetail bucks. And the nod in many instances goes to the bowhunter who gets to start pursuing deer before gun hunters. Being a bowhunter is a particular benefit if you live in an area where you can spend considerable time scouting deer. Locate him before he changes his routine and hunt him.

The best time to take big mature deer is the first legal opportunity you have to do so.

Colorado, through their Ranching for Wildlife Program, allows land managers to establish their own seasons, within certain parameters. That means the season on a particular chunk of eastern Colorado under this program can open in mid-September when bucks are still in bachelor herds and in their late summer patterns. On the opposite of those seasons, they can extend late enough to encompass the majority of the whitetail rut.

To become part of this program the landowner has to grant access to a certain number of public hunters, tags which are issued through a lottery-style drawing. Should you be lucky enough to draw a tag in a particularly good area, you are nearly assured of taking a quality deer.

In some states such as Iowa there is also a late muzzleloader season, which as this is being written also runs concurrent with a handgun season (regulations require using a straight-walled cartridge). If you are so fortunate as to draw a tag for this season, the chances are excellent of taking a monstrous-size buck. As mentioned I've been fortunate to draw late muzzleloader tags in the past. These days I apply so I'll be able to hunt with a handgun; unfortunately thus far I've been unsuccessful. But one of these days!

Special seasons and access to special areas can change from time to time. If you are truly interested in hunting these types of seasons, and you definitely should be, the best way to keep abreast of these seasons is by contacting the state wildlife agencies or departments of natural resources in the states that truly interest you. (The websites are listed in the Appendix.)

Larry Weishuhn's Remington Model XP-100 took down this 11-point buck during the extra opportunity offered by a special handgun season.

Plan for Success

Outfitted hunts can produce quality trophies like this long-tined eight-pointer. When interviewing an outfitter, ask about the current deer density and herd composition in the area that you plan to hunt.

East

The East is full of great white-tailed deer hunting opportunities but to be successful you must put some time into planning your hunts. Besides, this is a fun part of the hunt. Whether your hunt is at your hunting club near home, a wildlife management area a state away, or that fully outfitted dream hunt you have been saving for, planning is a must if the hunt is to have a reasonable chance for success.

In all cases weather, moon phases, terrain, rutting dates, deer density, hunting techniques, and equipment selection must be taken into consideration for any hunt to be fun and rewarding. If you are hunting near home, planning can be a little more relaxed as you already know much that goes into planning. Besides, if things don't go right it's not far to the house and tomorrow can be another day. However, if you are hunting far from home, things had better be well planned.

Let's look first at the fully outfitted eastern hunt. More and more hunters are selecting these hunts especially if that dream buck is what they are after. For many hunters, due to the cost and time off the job, this is a once-in-a-lifetime hunt. It better go right.

THE OUTFITTED HUNT

Bob Cox was an avid whitetail hunter. Every free moment he had during the local deer season was spent hunting. His best buck was an eight-pointer that scored 125 B&C points. His fondest dream was to go on an outfitted hunt where he'd have a chance of taking a buck scoring 140 or better.

After years of saving, Cox finally had enough money in his special savings account to take his dream hunt. Now it was time to select an outfitter. Having no experience at booking outfitted hunts, Cox began his search by picking out three whitetail hunt ads from his favorite hunting magazine. Each had a large ad with a hunter posing with a trophy-class buck. One ad was from an outfit in Canada, one from Alabama, and one from the Ohio Valley. Cox knew all three areas offered good hunting. He placed a call to each outfitter.

He tried calling the first outfitter several times, but each time he got a child on the phone and no one returned his calls. The second outfitter was a matter-of-fact talking fellow who promised Cox that if he hunted with him for five days, he would get a chance at a buck scoring 130 points or better, and with some luck, he might get a shot at a 140-plus buck.

However, the outfitter warned him if he couldn't make a 250-yard shot, he could come home empty-handed. Cox wrote this outfitter off as a farmer trying to pick up a few extra bucks as a guide.

The third call Cox made was to a lodge that outfitted whitetail hunts. Cox got a salesman on the phone. He assured Cox that if he booked a hunt with that lodge, he would get his buck. "We're running a 70 percent success rate," the enthusiastic voice on the other end of the phone told him. "Our lodge is as comfortable as your favorite hotel, and the food here is out of this world." Cox was sold. Easy hunting, plush accommodations, and lots of good food. He sent in his 50 percent deposit.

One week before the scheduled hunt, Cox called the hunt salesman to see who would pick him up at the airport. The friendly salesman told him a van was available for airport pickup, but it would cost an additional $75 above the $300 per day hunt cost. Surprise number one.

At long last Cox's dream hunt had become a reality. He arrived at the lodge to find it just as the salesman had told him— plush. After a hearty lunch, the chief guide called everyone into a room for a briefing. There were 20 other hunters in the group. Few were serious hunters; it was a group being entertained by a company. They were more interested in opening the bar and setting up the poker table.

During the short briefing, Cox learned that the method of hunting wouldn't be stalking as he preferred, but he would be hunting from a permanent ground blind sitting next to a food plot.

Following the briefing, Cox got into a truck with five other hunters. Their driver was also their guide. When the truck got to a muddy side road, the guide stopped and told Cox his blind was down the road and on the edge of a half-acre food plot. Cox was left standing in the road as the truck sped away.

He didn't walk far down the old road until he came to a stretch that was under 6 inches of water. No one had told him to prepare to wade, and his boots weren't waterproof.

Finally, with soaked, cold feet, he crawled into the boxlike blind. It was obvious by all the soft drink cans, candy wrappers, and cigarette butts that the blind was used often. On the walls were written passages such as "Nov. 19—No deer!" and "Dec. 3— Supposed to be peak of the rut, saw one small doe."

Be discriminating when choosing a fully outfitted hunt.

His enthusiasm waned. That afternoon he saw two does walk across the small plot. Nothing else. He wished he were stalk hunting.

That night, while the dinner was good, he was left out of the conversation as the others talked about their business. Later, Cox got little sleep as the group partied all night.

At daybreak he was back in the same blind with feet soaked and cold. This time he saw no deer. His guide insisted that he be back at the pickup point at 10:30, even though Cox wanted to stay out all day. The afternoon was the same as before. None of the other hunters were seeing bucks either. They didn't seem to care.

After two more days of this, Cox met with the chief guide and expressed his dissatisfaction with the hunt. During his meeting, he learned the 70 percent success rate the hunt salesman had promoted was not for bucks, but bucks and does combined. Also, he learned that due to the hunting pressure put on the lodge property, very few bucks taken scored over 130 points. Cox's dream hunt was falling apart.

The guide would not allow Cox to stalk hunt. "Against company policy" he was told, but the guide did agree to put him in a different blind. On the last afternoon of the hunt, Cox finally saw a small seven-point buck which, out of desperation, he took. At the lodge, he learned that there would be extra fees for skinning and butchering the deer. Also, an ice chest suitable for taking the meat home cost Cox twice as much at the lodge as it would anywhere else. Cox returned home devastated, and it took him months to get over his "once-in-a-lifetime" hunt.

Use a phone, combined with a map, to interview prospective outfitters.

Selecting an outfitter for your dream hunt should be done with great care. While there are many excellent whitetail outfitters in business to give you a great hunt, there are also a number of outfitters who will take your money and disappoint you. Your search should begin by coming up with a list of outfitters in the area you wish to hunt.

One source of outfitters' names is the "Guides and Outfitters" section of outdoor magazines. But don't assume that just because an outfitter has an ad in a magazine that he is reputable; it simply means he had enough money to pay for an enticing ad. Select those outfitters whose ads appeal to you to add to your list of hunting operations to check out.

The best way to learn about outfitters is from friends who have actually used the outfitter's services within the last two years. Many excellent whitetailed deer outfitters run small operations, and thanks to their efforts to run a good service, need little or no advertising. Word of mouth from satisfied hunters keeps them booked well in advance.

Once you select a list of outfitters, begin checking them out at least a year in advance of your planned hunt. When I was a whitetail outfitter, each year a number of hunters simply appeared at the lodge without reservations or called at the last minute to book a hunt, and were always surprised that the lodge was fully booked months in advance. Write to each outfitter requesting his literature. This will give you some general information to study on each operation and help you ask specific questions when you go to the next step of the selection process, a phone conversation with each outfitter that you have selected.

Why phone rather than writing or e-mailing? If you send the outfitters a list of 25 questions that require two or three hours of their time to answer, chances are you won't get many responses. Most hunting operations are small businesses and time simply doesn't allow for most outfitters to spend hours answering each potential hunter's questions by mail. Most outfitters prefer a call from someone who is wellprepared for the interview.

The best way to conduct a phone interview with outfitters is with a written list of questions. This way you will not omit some important questions, and after all the interviews are complete, you can compare answers from each outfitter.

Begin your phone interview by introducing yourself and telling the outfitter where you are from. Next, make sure he has time for you to ask him some questions about his hunts. Tell him up-front if you want to hunt with a bow, muzzleloader, handgun, modern rifle, or shotgun. If you have any physical limitations that would require you to hunt in a specific way, you should let him know early in the conversation. The more he knows about you, the better he can inform you about the services he can or cannot offer.

Then it's time to start asking your questions. Where does he hunt? What is the terrain like in that area? What is the weather like during the time you want to hunt? When does the peak of rut usually occur? What hunting techniques are used — drives, elevated stands, ground blinds, elevated tower on a truck? What are the physical demands of the hunt? Will you have a guide with you? If so, how many hunters per guide? Will he or someone else guide you? What is their experience? How long has he outfitted white-tailed deer hunts? In the area you want to hunt? How many hunters does he take at one time? What are the lodge or camp accommodations? How many actual hunting days are included? What is the cost of the hunt? Exactly what does that cover? What does it not cover? What are his deposit and cancellation policies? What about transportation between the airport and the camp? Who arranges it, and is there an additional charge? Is there an additional charge for skinning, butchering, and preparing a trophy for the trip home? What other additional expenses can you expect? Is there a trophy fee? What equipment is the hunter expected to furnish?

Ask for the name and address of three hunters who hunted with him last year and were successful, then three who were not successful. Finally, what was the hunter success rate on mature bucks last year? The last five years? Hunter success rates will often tell you a lot about an outfitter. If he will exaggerate on this important information, he will usually mislead you on other facts. What were the Boone & Crockett scores on the bucks? Most outfitters will be honest with you, but there are exceptions.

Think back to the second outfitter Cox called. While Cox did not like his matter-of-fact answers, he was probably a good outfitter, giving Cox straight answers, while the corporate salesman sounded good but gave misleading and incomplete information.

Thank the outfitter for his time and tell him you will get back with him after you check out his references.

The next step is where many hunters fail. They don't call the references. Take the time to call each reference and ask prepared questions. Begin by introducing yourself and ask permission to discuss their hunts with Big Buck Outfitter. Ask these questions:

How would he or she rate the overall hunt? Was he successful? If so, what was the Boone & Crockett score of the buck's

A deer hunter takes aim from a permanently installed tree stand on a hunting lease in a Southeast forest. When interviewing an outfitter, find out what hunting techniques he uses and what the terrain is like in his area.

When checking out a new hunting area, get to know the local wildlife biologist and conservation officer. They will be able to provide a wealth of information about terrain, cover, browse and hunting conditions in their district.

antlers? How many mature bucks did they see? What hunting technique was used? How many hunters were in camp? How was the lodging? Food? Guides? Equipment? Was there enough help in camp? Was the hunt well organized and safe? Were there hidden or unexpected costs? What was the terrain like? Weather? Who was their guide? How would they rate him? What did they not like about the hunt? What equipment did they not have that they wish they had taken? Would they hunt with this outfitter again? Get this information from six hunters, and you will have a good idea of the quality of the service. Now you can decide whether or not you will want to spend hundreds or thousands of dollars and some valuable hunting time with him.

Keep in mind during your evaluation that the most important consideration is whether the outfitter hunts the way you want to hunt. Many outfitters run excellent hunting operations but might not employ the hunting methods you prefer.

Once you decide on an outfitter, you should call him right away to let him know your decision and planned dates. This is especially true when planning a hunt a year or more in the future. Ask for a contract spelling out the details of the hunt, including deposit, cancellation clause, and when the balance for the hunt is due.

At the same time, you should send the outfitter a letter spelling out your understanding of your arrival and departure times and dates, total cost of the hunt, deposit and final payment, including amount, date due, and method of payment. Many outfitters require a cashier's check for the final payment. Stay in touch with the outfitter, especially if your hunt is several months away. Outfitters lose their leases, go bankrupt, die, etc., and you should look after your deposit, as well as get to know him better. You will learn quickly when you check out outfitters that some of the best ones fill up quickly and may be booked years in advance. If so, ask to be placed on his waiting list. During the years I was in the outfitting business, I was booked one to two years in advance; however, I maintained a waiting list to fill canceled hunts.

If Bob Cox had taken the time to check out the three outfitters he was interested in hunting with, he, no doubt wouldn't have selected the one he hunted with. An outfitted hunt is expensive, but when you are hunting with the right outfitter it really can be a dream hunt.

THE DO-IT-YOURSELF HUNT

The do-it-yourself hunt may be a few miles from your home or in another state but there needs to be a lot of planning before the hunt. Needless to say if you have any choice in planning your hunting dates you will do some simple research to try to avoid being on the hunt when the moon is bright, the weather is bad, the rut is over, or going on a weekend hunt to get there and find there is no Sunday hunting. With the exception of the weather, most of these things can be checked out early in the planning process.

If you are going to a public hunting area, such as a state wildlife management area, military base, state forest, or timber company lands, go to the trouble to find out the name of the local wildlife manager and give him or a staff member a call to find out detailed information. In a short conversation you can find out about deer densities, buck harvest data, terrain, vegetative cover, rut dates, hunting techniques that work best, how to dress for the hunt, recommended firearms, information about camping and accommodations, costs, special regulations, and much more. Keep notes and be sure to thank this person for they have just done a lot of planning for you.

If you are going into an area to hunt private land, find out how to contact the local state wildlife biologist and give him a call requesting the same information. I have always found these people to be glad to help when properly approached. Many years ago, I was one of these people and I was proud I could be of help to out-of-state hunters, as long as they weren't demanding and didn't take too much time telling me their hunting stories.

Next, obtain maps of the area and learn them well. A topo map of your hunting area can give you a lot of planning information and get you somewhat familiar with the terrain before you leave home.

Fortunately, in the East there are good accommodations near most deer hunting areas. Whether you are camping or staying at a motel it is easy to check out their quality and make reservations in advance. If you are planning on eating at restaurants it is a good idea to check into their operating hours, both for breakfast and dinner, as in many small towns they may be closed when you need their service.

The most valuable tool I use for my hunts is a what-to-take list. I make one for every hunt I go on. This list includes every item I will take on the hunt including obvious items such as toiletries, extra cash, hunt license, glasses, etc. I am always surprised at hunters who arrive in camp

and will have forgotten the most basic items. Some items go with me no matter what. Regardless of where I hunt, my rain suit and long johns go, even on summer groundhog hunts. List the caliber of rifle and ammo. It is embarrassing to arrive in camp with your pet 7mm-08 and two boxes of .30-06 ammo.

I make it a point to carry the regulations of the area I am going to hunt. First, they should be read long before the hunt and next if a question comes up during the

hunt you have a quick reference.

The hunter who arrives in camp well organized, has lots of knowledge of the area and deer habits, is rested, and with the right gear for the hunt has more time to devote to the hunt and usually he will be the hunter who fills his tag.

Regardless of what type eastern deer hunt you go on, don't depend upon someone else to do your homework and hunt planning. Good detail planning puts the odds for success on you.

Careful pre-hunt planning, attention to detail, and a Thompson Center carbine gave Wayne Fears the edge in taking this Texas 10-pointer.

West

Many a hunter's dream has come true on a western hunt, but unfortunately some dreams can turn into nightmares. The difference often comes about in how hunts are approached and what you consider reasonable expectation. Deer throughout much of the West tend to produce really nice antlers, "big" when compared to the average racks taken in much of the eastern half of the continent. But not all western whitetails are huge nor are big bucks always plentiful.

Over the past many years as an outdoor writer, wildlife biologist, and television show producer, I have spent many days in hunting camps throughout the western side of our continent in search of whitetails. I have also spent quite a bit of time in hunting camps as guide and hunt manager. During those years I have listened to tales of great bucks bested, as well as the laments of hunters whose hunts of a lifetime had gone awry.

Recently I was approached by a hunter in the Dallas/Fort Worth airport. He was haggard looking, obviously tired, and headed home from a tough whitetail trip in western Canada. "Know the very best part of the trip I'm coming home from?" he asked. Then before I could even consider a reply he continued, "All the dreaming I did about the deer I

would see and the big buck I would take." Then shaking his head he again spoke, "I should have saved my money, hunted near home, at least in Texas I could have seen and possibly taken a deer! I spent seven days sitting in a tree stand in below zero weather, couldn't eat the sandwiches nor candy bars the cook gave me because they were frozen solid, hunted from before first light until dark and then waited a couple of hours each night before the guide picked me up. Never saw a deer the entire hunt. I'll never go back!" he said as he headed toward his gate.

I knew how he felt. I had experienced the same hunt in the past in a different part of Canada. I had saved for a long time to hunt Canadian whitetail and my hunt was set up as a guided hunt, with meals and lodging provided. The outfitter/guide told me the most successful way to hunt the area was from a tree stand, which he had taken the liberty to erect where two rub and scrape lines met.

Each morning, well before daylight, I was dropped off at the foot of my tree stand and instructed to crawl up and wait there until dark when I would be picked up. That first morning, driving to where I was to hunt, I failed to see any deer tracks in the freshly fallen snow. That should have been a harbinger of things to come.

From my perch I could glass a fair amount of real estate, but nary a track, nor rub did I see, all the while thinking perhaps the fresh snow had covered all traces of any scrapes in the area.

Each day of the hunt the routine was the same, be driven to the stand without seeing any tracks crossing the road. Sit and stand all day long in frigid temperatures, try to eat frozen sandwiches, watch for deer to no avail, be picked up no less than an hour after dark, then drive back to camp while failing to see any deer tracks crossing the snow-covered road. For four days I did just like my guide said, after all I was hunting in his home territory and I had spent good money to take advantage of his expertise.

Even though there was little time to talk to others in camp, about the fourth night it became apparent that no one else in camp was seeing any deer, nor had they seen any fresh tracks.

The outfitter had come highly recommended from a friend who had hunted with him three years previously. All in camp had taken bucks scoring 150 B&C or better that year, the biggest being a mid-170s B&C deer. Even bigger bucks had been seen and/or missed.

I finally confronted the outfitter with my thoughts about the area, based on what I and others had failed to see. He confessed that during the previous year the area we hunted had had a tremendously severe winter die-off. "To be honest with you, it would surprise me if you did see a deer on this hunt." I wish he had imparted some of that "honesty" before the hunt.

I was not pleased with the outfitter. He had not told me about the die-off. But neither was I pleased with myself. I should have checked on such a possibility before agreeing to make the trip. The fault for the unsuccessful hunt and expensive lesson lay as much in my court as it did his.

OUTFITTED, GUIDED, AND SELF-GUIDED HUNTS

Most of us enamored with hunting whitetails dream of taking that once-in-a-lifetime hunt, where everything goes right and we end up tagging a monstrous buck. Can such hunts truly become a reality? Obviously they do happen because each year thousands of deer hunters go on guided and unguided hunts and indeed do return home with

Thorough homework before a guided hunt can ensure the "dream hunt of a lifetime" rather than a nightmare.

sizable whitetail bucks.

Dream hunt of a lifetime or just another nightmare? How can you distinguish between the two before they happen and what can we do to have all the factors in our favor? The answer is neither simple nor easy. In the case of the hunt just described I had done most everything right. The area I had chosen to hunt had previously produced some extremely big bucks; friends and acquaintances had hunted with the outfitter and returned with not only good deer, but also glowing reports how the outfitter had gone beyond what was expected of him to make their hunts successful. The only thing missing was deer!

The best way to ensure a successful and fun hunt is to do your homework before you commit to any particular whitetail hunt, whether guided or even unguided. The price of the hunt either extremely high or exceptionally low won't ensure your success rate or hunting pleasure. With white-tailed deer hunting you don't always get what you pay for.

QUESTIONS TO ASK

In an earlier chapter I stated I enjoyed hunting mature bucks, those four and half years old or older. Thus the questions I ask of outfitters or hunting ranches are designed around that goal. I realize some outfitters

An outfitter's crew dresses out a client's buck. Remember to ask about additional costs such as meat care.

ment programs if properly established and maintained start showing positive results about the fifth or sixth year, as young deer born into the program start maturing and show up in harvest data.

What is the current deer density and herd composition?

The deer density should be expressed in acres per deer. Information about herd composition should include current buck to doe ratios, fawn survival rates, what percentage of the bucks surveyed, if indeed a deer census has been performed, have eight or more points, and what percentage in the biologist's opinion are four years old or older. Remember mature bucks tend to produce larger racks than do younger bucks.

Deer density depending upon the area can vary from perhaps somewhere of one deer per 10 to 20 acres to as low a population as approximately a deer per 50 to 75 acres. In the case of the latter I know not to expect to see too many deer.

In terms of buck to doe ratios, I much prefer to hunt where the buck to doe ratio is one buck per three does or narrower. Because that means there are more bucks present.

I'll want to know and pay particular attention to what kind of fawn crop there was four, five, six, and seven years ago. This information is important because, unless there was a heavy harvest in the past, there should be a goodly number of mature deer in the herd if fawn survival rates were 50 percent or higher during those past years.

might not be able to provide answers to all the questions, but they can certainly answer those they know something about. Some of the questions I ask include the following:

What size is the hunting area? Is the property under a long-term wildlife management program, and if so who administers and evaluates the management plan and its progress? How do I get in touch with that individual?

Size in some instances might not be overly important, but in some instances it could be, especially if the property is extremely small or on the large side.

If indeed the property is under a management program I want to speak to the individual in charge to find out as much as I can. Hopefully the person in charge will be a wildlife biologist. Among other things I will want to know how long the management program has been in existence. Most manage-

How many bucks are taken from the area you plan to hunt each year, and how many were two or three years of age? Photos of the bucks taken should give you an idea of their average ages, antler measurement, and body sizes. How many of the bucks taken were over four years of age?

Most good hunting operations maintain annual records of the bucks harvested on lands under their control. Look for those places where the average age falls within the parameters of the type of deer you're looking for and hoping to take.

If the average age of bucks taken is two or three years old, it means that part of the bucks taken were likely yearlings while others were older, or a large number of the bucks taken indeed were only two or three years of age.

Average antler measurements, particularly total number of points, main beam lengths, base circumferences and inside spread will give you a pretty good idea of the quality of bucks taken. Many hunting operations now also can supply you with gross Boone & Crockett scores of the bucks they take each year.

When are the best bucks taken in the area?

Some hunting areas tend to produce their best bucks early, while they are still in their late summer patterns. Other places produce their best bucks right before the rut when bucks are on the prowl and have a tendency to respond to rattling horns. If you're interested in rattling up deer, ask when the tail end of the pre-rut occurs. Still other areas produce their biggest deer during the rut when bucks are actively chasing does. And some areas tend to produce a few big bucks after the peak of the rut is over, when there is great competition for what few does remain.

Has the area you plan to hunt experienced a recent severe winter or summer die-off? Has the area experienced a recent outbreak of bluetongue (EHD) or other diseases?

Earlier I mentioned the experience I had in Manitoba several years ago, where the extremely harsh and long winter previous to my hunt pretty well killed off all the deer in the area.

On another occasion I was preparing for a long-awaited hunt in one of the midwestern states. A couple of weeks before I was to leave, I called both the local wildlife biologist and the warden in the area I planned to hunt. According to them EHD (a viral disease, sometimes called bluetongue) had swept through the area and had killed many deer. During the summer of 2001 just north of where I live in Southwest Texas there was a devastating die-off in the area's whitetails due to an anthrax outbreak. Anthrax is endemic to the region, found in the soil since the days when buffalo roamed the area.

Chronic Wasting Disease (CWD) is something we will have to deal with in the future. In my opinion it's been here forever, but we're just now learning about it. Unfortunately, perception and reality are often two totally different things. I do not see CWD as a problem, but unfortunately some others do. If you are concerned, call and ask before you hunt an area.

TIPS FOR TRAVELING WITH FIREARMS

If traveling by air, show up early. Although check-in times have been reduced lately, some travelers have experienced three-hour delays from curbside to gate.

Check the requirements of your airline ahead of time to avoid surprises. When checking a firearm, you must declare to the ticket counter representative that you are checking a weapon. If there is a security checkpoint before the ticket counter, you must declare the existence of a weapon to security personnel. Present your firearms unloaded and sign a "firearms unloaded" declaration, to be placed inside the gun case. The gun must be locked in a hard-sided, crushproof container.

Ensure that any ammunition is packed in the manufacturer's original package or securely packed in fiber, wood or metal boxes, which will be packed in your checked luggage. F.A.A. regulations limit ammunition to 11 pounds, with some airlines specifying less. If you are a muzzleloader hunter, caps and loose powder are not allowed. Also, be careful about packing clothes and equipment near your loading bench. Minute traces of powder residue could contaminate your gear and set off some of the more sophisticated hi-tech explosive detection devices.

An alternative is to ship your guns ahead via UPS or Federal Express to a licensed gun dealer in the area you will be hunting.

If hunting in a foreign country, maintain entry permits in your possession for the country or countries of destination or transit. Firearms possession permits are required for all Mexico- and Canada-bound hunters.

Photograph your firearms and keep a record of their serial numbers. If a gun is stolen or lost by an airline, a photo is handy for identification. Guns should be insured if they exceed an airline's limit of liability.

Invest in a metal gun case fitted with a crossbar that locks with a padlock. These cases are worth the added expense and will outlast lower priced hard plastic models.

When packing a gun in an airline-approved hard case, place the gun in a padded soft gun case to add some extra protection. Some states require that guns be cased while in a vehicle, and a soft case is more convenient.

Pack your gun with the bottom of the gun toward the gun case's hinge. If a careless baggage handler drops your gun case and the gun slides to the bottom, the sights or scope won't strike the hinge's hard inner surface.

Tape all of your gun case latches to keep them from becoming snagged on baggage conveyors after you fill out a firearm declaration card.

It's a good idea to attach a laminated card with your name and address to the outside of your gun case. Include your name and address to the inside of the case as a backup.

Keep gun cases and guns out of sight when possible. Locked hotel rooms are a safer bet than securing them in a vehicle.

Carry an extra scope and set of rings. Scopes can be damaged in transit or in the field. Having a spare handy can save a hunt.

Meticulous planning lets Larry Weishuhn go on every hunt expecting success like this southeastern 10-pointer.

Ask about reasonable expectations. What kind of buck can you really expect to take?

Most of us interested in whitetails are hoping to take good bucks when we go hunting, likely the best bucks of our lifetime. But that does not happen very often. So try to determine what size buck you can reasonably expect to take while hunting. Know going into a hunt what you can expect. Be careful of those who promise the moon and then likely cannot even deliver moonlight. Again, ask for references and then ask for proof in terms of photos.

Going into most hunts I have a pretty good idea of the type of buck I'm looking for. I normally hunt for mature deer or at least deer representative of what the area can produce. If the best I can reasonably expect is a buck in the 130 B&C class, then I'm going to be happy with taking such a deer. But I also don't want to take the first 130-class buck I see if there is a reasonable expectation of taking a 150 or better.

Find out what is included in the price of the hunt before you get there! Does it include meals, lodging, and guide? How about transportation to and from the nearest airport? Is caping and care for the meat included, how about the cost of a container to ship the meat home? Are there any hidden costs,

and if so what are they?

Most outfitters/guides these days pretty well spell out what all is included in the cost of their hunts. But it's important to ask the questions mentioned. Don't be caught by surprises. If you know the costs ahead of time and exactly what is and what is not included you are not going to be caught short.

By working through a legitimate and reputable booking agent who is long in experience a lot of the problems you might otherwise encounter seldom materialize.

How will you hunt, from permanent stands, spot and stalk? What weather can you expect? Are waterproof boots and raingear necessary?

Taking the right clothing is sometimes as important as taking the right gun. If you're in a tree stand, or for that matter stalking and wearing the wrong boots and clothing, life can be miserable. The same is true if you're prepared for dry weather and are confronted with cold rain and mud puddles. The best advice about what to bring in terms of a hunting trip is to be prepared for a variety of weather conditions, both in terms of the proper clothing and gear and also to be mentally prepared for whatever type of weather is sent your way.

How far will my "normal" shot be?

To someone who has hunted western whitetails, a 300-yard or longer shot might be simply another day at the office. But to someone not used to long-range shooting, it might be an impossible shot.

While on a hunt in eastern Wyoming there were two other hunters in camp. One was from Pennsylvania and the other from North Carolina. Both were on their first western deer hunt. The Pennsylvanian brought his favorite deer rifle, an open-sighted Winchester Model 94 chambered for the .30-30. He mentioned he felt comfortable taking a shot out to about a hundred yards. The hunter from North Carolina carried a bolt-action .270 Winchester topped with a Leupold variable scope.

Unfortunately neither of the two killed a deer. The .30-30 hunter only saw bucks at about 250 yards or farther away. To his credit he did not shoot. When the hunt was over he vowed to return the next year, properly armed and ready for long-distance shooting.

The .270 hunter had numerous potential opportunities at bucks only about 150 to 200 yards away, but proclaimed the shots were far too long for him. Back home where he had previously hunted a 75-yard shot was considered "long." Even though he had purchased the .270 specifically for the western hunt where he had been told by the outfitter shots could be long, he refused to shoot because he thought he would not be able to hit a deer at the 150- to 200- yard distances.

Questioned if he had previously even shot the .270 at the range at distances of 100 yards or beyond, he replied "Nope!" He went home disappointed, vowing never to return.

A bit of homework and range time could have turned their disappointing hunt into a roaring success. Be prepared for the type of shooting that may be expected of you and spend time at the range shooting both from the bench and in field position. Practice using shooting sticks and learn how to take advantage of natural rests such as limbs, boulders, or even packframes. Practice at short and long ranges, and at ranges well beyond the distances you ever expect to take a deer.

If you are not familiar with hunting in open country, get a rangefinder, because out West distance can certainly fool you.

PHYSICAL CONDITIONING AND PROPER ATTITUDE

Being physically prepared can make a lot of difference regarding your enjoyment on a western whitetail hunt. While most of the time even out West whitetail hunting is done either by sitting on stands, spending considerable time glassing and then spotting and stalking, there can be quite a bit of walking involved and if you are hunting the foothills, a bit of rough walking. If your outfitter or the topo maps you've gathered of the self-guided area suggest that there may be a lot of walking, get in shape before going on the hunt.

A few years ago I was on a western Canadian whitetail hunt where all we did from first to last light was do long and involved deer drives. Thankfully I was in pretty good shape going into the hunt, the result of several mountain hunts earlier in the fall. Unfortunately one of my friends from Dallas who accompanied me had spent most of his summer and early fall behind a desk. Each night when we would finally get back to camp, he was dead tired and muscle sore. Even though he finally took a nice deer, I'm sure it wasn't one of his most enjoyable hunts.

Both from a personal perspective and as an observer in many different hunting camps I am convinced the difference between hunting success and failure is quite often having the "proper" attitude. I go into every hunt fully expecting to have a fabulous time. I try to maintain that attitude regardless of what happens.

I have seen many hunts ruined for individuals because they put too much pressure on themselves to take a monster buck. When you go on a whitetail hunt do so to enjoy the entire hunt, including the time in camp with fellow hunters. Get involved in camp life, offer to help wash dishes and possibly even do some cooking. It's great to be waited on hand and foot but it's even more fun to get involved with the camp.

We all want to be on the hunt where conditions are perfect, including the weather and deer activity. It doesn't always happen, but don't let that destroy the fun and the thrill of the hunt.

I go on every hunt expecting to be successful. But I also go on hunts knowing I'm going to have a great time.

Whitetail Guns

Smoke billows from Wayne Fears' .50 caliber Knight in-line. Some of Fears' most memorable and challenging deer hunts have been muzzleloading rifle hunts.

East

The wind blew large, heavy snowflakes into the dense Michigan cedar swamp where I was deer hunting. I was cold but excited about slowly stalking along a well-used deer trail that wound through the thick brush in the swamp. For this hunt, I had brought my Ruger 77 in a .280 Rem. As I picked my way between two snow-laden cedars, I saw a large eight-point buck standing looking the opposite way in a small opening only 20 yards away. With my heart racing, I started to mount my rifle, but the barrel caught in the thick limbs around me. Seconds later and after much more movement, I got my rifle mounted, but by then the buck had bolted. I looked through the scope but it was set on six power and all I could find was brush. I was brush hunting with a rifle that was best suited for long-range shooting. It cost me a nice buck. How I wished I had brought my Marlin 1895G Guide Gun with me on this trip.

The eastern half of North America offers the white-tailed deer hunter a wide variety of terrain and habitat features that must be considered when he selects his firearm. In some cases the type of firearm and load may be dictated by regulations, such as shotgun with slug load or muzzleloading rifle only. However, in most cases it is up to the hunter to select the firearm he wishes to use.

Hunting conditions can vary from thick brush where shots may not be over 20 yards to vast open areas, such as clear-cuts or agricultural fields, where shots may be 300 or more yards. There are situations where cover and shot distances can change, difficult for the stalk hunter who may go through several of these varying areas in one day.

CALIBER

Due to the varying ranges an eastern deer hunter is likely to encounter, he must have some idea of what the downrange energy level of a bullet must be to cleanly kill a deer when selecting the caliber of his deer rifle. He should also know how far downrange that energy level is maintained in any caliber he is considering using. This is the effective killing range of that caliber on white-tailed deer.

In order to recommend a minimum energy level for white-tailed deer caliber selection, I have studied standards set by those who have researched the effects of kinetic energy on wild animals. The standard that came closest to my own experience as a wildlife professional and hunter was found in *Handbook for Shooters and Reloaders*, a book by well-known gun expert P. O. Ackley. In a chapter on killing power, the standard for energy levels that a cartridge must provide on deer-size game was set at 1200 foot-pounds. Remember this is not muzzle energy, but retained energy at the target.

Commonly accepted white-tailed deer calibers ranging from .243 Winchester to .45-70 Government shooting factory loads have downrange energy levels of this amount at varying ranges.

Those hunting in thick brush where distances to the target are close might consider the .257 Roberts (117-grain bullet) which maintains the 1200 foot-pounds of energy out to 140 yards; the .30-30

Winchester (150-grain bullet) out to 120 yards; the .35 Remington (200-grain bullet) out to 115 yards; the .450 Marlin (350-grain bullet) out to 250 yards; and the .45-70 Government (405-grain bullet) out to 110 yards.

Rifles in these calibers are commonly called "brush rifles," and it is a common misconception that they are called brush rifles because bullets in these calibers can strike brush and stay on course. Don't you believe it! No bullet is capable of doing that. These rifles are called "brush rifles" due to their short effective range; and rifles in these calibers often have short barrels for easy maneuverability in thick brush.

I will never forget the first ten-point buck I ever had the opportunity to take. It was early in my hunting days, and I had been sold on the idea that the .30-30 Win could shoot accurately through light brush. I had saved my money and bought a .30-30 Win in a Winchester Model 94. After taking several small bucks with the rifle, I got on the trail of a large buck that was feeding late in the afternoon in a large field planted in winter wheat. One evening I crawled up on a mound of dirt that was grown up in weeds at one end of the field. There, just 75 yards in front of me stood a beautiful ten-point buck. My heart raced. Lying on my stomach, I eased the rifle up only to see grass and weeds in front of the muzzle. Nevertheless, I did not worry; I had been told that the .30-30 Model 94 was a brush rifle that would shoot through light brush. I took a good sight picture on the buck, held my breath, and squeezed the trigger. At the crack of the rifle, the buck exited the field with fleeting leaps. My heart sank. The grass and weeds had deflected the bullet. The next day my hunting partner got the buck. I learned the truth about brush rifles the hard way.

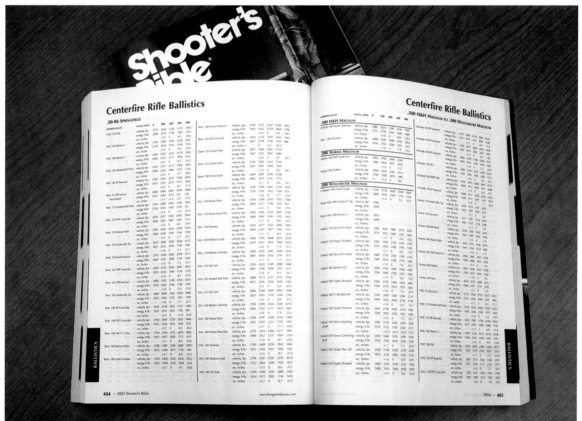

Ballistics charts, found in ammunition manufacturer's catalogs or websites, are valuable tools in understanding the downrange energy of loads and the performance of your firearm with different ammunition.

The wide variety of cartridges available greatly increases the chance of success with a long-range shot.

The T/C Contender Carbine offers a compact action, making it ideal for hunting in brush or thick cover.

Hunters in open woods or around small fields where distances to the target are around 250 yards will want to consider rifles in such calibers as .243 Winchester (100-grain bullet), which maintains the 1200 foot-pounds of energy out to 250 yards; 6mm Remington (100-grain bullet) out to 300 yards; .25-06 Remington (100-grain bullet) out to 285 yards; 7x57 (140-grain bullet) out to 325 yards; .300 Savage (150-grain bullet) out to 280 yards; and the .308 Winchester (150-grain bullet) out to 345 yards.

Those hunters who hunt vast openings, such as clear-cuts, agricultural fields, gas or power line rights-of-way, or from mountainside to mountainside will want to consider the .270 Winchester (130-grain bullet) which maintains the 1200 foot-pound energy level out to 435 yards; the 7mm-08 Remington (140-grain bullet) out to 410 yards; the .280 Remington (150-grain bullet) out to 435 yards; the 7mm Remington Magnum (150-grain bullet) out to 485 yards; or the .30-06 Springfield (150-grain bullet) out to 435 yards.

ACTION

A hunter's method of hunting usually has a lot to do with the rifle action he selects for white-tailed deer. A hunter who does most of his hunting from a stable, permanent blind adjacent to an open field may choose a single-shot action such as a Ruger No. 1, H & R Handi-Rifle or the T/C Encore or the T/C Contender. These rifles are very short due to the compactness of the action so they are easily maneuvered in a confined space, yet they can have long barrels and long-range accuracy. In this situation, one-shot kills are relatively easy so there is less often a need for a quick second shot. Stand hunters who hunt in open timber with little understory vegetation frequently choose this action as well.

Hunters who like to go on dog drives, and some who like man drives, where most of the shooting is a moving deer and where the need for a quick second or third shot may occur, the action of choice is the semi-automatic or pump. The Browning BAR, the Benelli R-1, and the Remington Model 7400 are popular semi-autos, and the Remington Model 7600 is a popular pump-action deer rifle.

Brush hunters often like lever action rifles such as the Winchester Model 94, Marlin 336, Marlin 1895, Marlin 444, and Browning Model 81. These rifles are usually available in short-range but effective calibers, are fast to use in confined stands, and have short overall length for easy maneuverability in brush.

The most popular action in the East is the bolt

The Marlin model 444 is a favorite
short-range deer rifle for hunters
hunting in thick brush.

action. Some of the best-known bolt actions are the Browning A-Bolt, Remington 700, Ruger M77, Sako, Savage 116, Weatherby Mark V, and Winchester Model 70. These well-known actions come in a variety of white-tailed deer calibers. Each of these actions has features such as unique safety designs, adjustable triggers, short bolt throw, etc. which make the bolt action a matter of personal preference.

Collectively, bolt-action rifles have a reputation for being accurate, safe, and relatively fast when a second shot is needed.

BARREL LENGTH

Barrel length has a lot to do with many eastern hunters' selection of their deer rifles. The 18^1/2- to 20-inch barrels are often the choice of hunters who stalk in thick brush or hunt from a permanent ground blind or portable tree stand. The Ruger No. 1 International, Savage Scout, Sako Carbine, Winchester Model 94, Ruger M77 International and Marlin 336 are just a few of the many rifles available in shorter barrel lengths.

The popular 24-inch barrel length is still the favorite of many deer hunters but there is a growing trend toward 22-inch barrels. They are short enough to be easy to maneuver in brush and blinds, yet long enough to give good muzzle velocity. A rapidly growing number of rifle models are available with 22-inch barrels, including the Browning BAR and A-Bolt, H&R Handi-Rifle, Remington 700, Model Seven, 7400, 7600, Ruger 77, Sako Hunter, and Winchester Model 70.

Modern deer hunters are blessed with a wide variety of available rifle designs and calibers, which can be matched to any terrain, habitat, or range that may be encountered. There are synthetic stocks for wet weather hunting, laminated stocks for rough country, camouflage stocks for stalking, and "Mannlicher-style" stocks for good looks and balance. The selection of the right caliber and rifle is simply a matter of the hunter giving some careful thought to his personal hunting preferences and matching it to his hunting area.

Bolt-action rifles, like this Remington-based custom
rifle, are the most popular actions for eastern hunts.

RIFLESCOPES

Where most rifles used in the West will be equipped with a riflescope, many in the East will have only open sights, a low-power riflescope, or a variable. This is due to the diverse ground cover and terrain. As many shots as not will be at close range, usually under 100 yards. Most of my short-range brush rifles are not equipped with scopes and I plan on keeping it that way.

Having said that, there is a place for riflescopes in the East; however, the rifle owner needs to give a lot of thought to where he hunts before plopping down some hard earned dollars for a scope. It is foolish to purchase a 3-12X50 variable riflescope if 99 percent of your hunting is in country where shots are not going to be over 150 yards. There have been a lot of top quality bucks escape to live another year because a hunter was over-scoped. On several occasions, I have missed an opportunity for a shot because the scope on my rifle was too powerful for a short-range shot. Think low power first and go up based on the longer ranges you are likely to shoot where you hunt. If most of your hunting is done in woods and food plots where most shots are inside 150 yards, consider variable riflescopes in the 1.5-5X or 2-7X range. If you can honestly say that a high percentage

Dave Henderson took this buck with a Browning Gold Deer Stalker. Modern shotguns, designed for deer hunting, are comparable to short-range rifles.

of your shots are going to be well over 150 yards, then consider the 3-9X or 4-12X scopes.

Today the hot talk is about getting a riflescope that gathers a lot of light for that dawn or dusk shot. Most hunters think they can achieve this by buying the largest objective lens they can find, usually a 50mm objective lens. This is only part of the solution. The main solution is to get a high-quality riflescope that is made to give maximum light transmission, prevents light diffusion, and has superior resolution and contrast. It will have multilayered-coated lens and will be nitrogen-filled. A large objective lens on a riflescope not having all these qualities will not let you see that buck sneaking into the food plot at dark well enough to get a clean shot. I trust names like Swarovski, Kahles, Zeiss, Leupold, Nikon, and Burris to give me this quality. I prefer to have a $600 scope on a $200 rifle than vice versa.

SHOTGUNS FOR EASTERN DEER HUNTING

There are a number of eastern states and special hunting areas, such as military bases, that require hunters to use only shotguns for deer hunting. There once was a time when there were limited choices of shot shell loads and shotguns designed specifically for deer hunting. However, this has all changed thanks to the development of sabot slug loads, rifled shotgun barrels, and shotgun scopes.

Today's deer shotgun can shoot 2-inch groups at 100 yards and take deer cleanly at distances not thought possible a few years ago. In fact, the modern slug loads can carry the 1200 foot-pound energy load of buck killing power out to 150 yards when shot from a 3-inch chambered 12-gauge rifled barrel. Furthermore, when equipped with a high-quality shotgun scope, slug shotguns like the Benelli M1 Field, Benelli Nova, Beretta AL391, Browning BPS, Remington 870 SPS, or Winchester 1300 will perform like rifles at moderate ranges.

As our human population density increases, we will see more shotgun-only hunts and these guns and loads are there to keep deer hunting fun and hunts successful.

MUZZLELOADERS FOR EASTERN DEER

Some of my most memorable and challenging deer hunts have been with muzzleloaders. When I began hunting with a muzzleloading rifle in the early 1970s most were shortrange firearms at best, often not very accurate, slow to load, a pain to clean, and there was always the question as to whether or not they would fire. High humidity and wet days encountered in the East made keeping one's powder dry a difficult chore.

Today we have muzzleloading rifles that are accurate out to 200 yards, easy to clean, fast to reload, dependable, and will take whitetails like a center fire rifle. Granted not every state or region will accept all the modern refinements, but where the latest in-lines are accepted, deer hunting with a muzzleloader is more efficient for everyone.

Serious whitetail hunters should use a high-quality riflescope that fits their usual hunting conditions.

Examples of Range in Yards at Which Cartridges Retain 1200 Ft.-Lb. Levels of Energy

CARTRIDGES	BULLET WEIGHT (GR.)	MUZZLE VELOCITY (FPS)	1200 FT.-LB. (YDS.)
.243 Win.	100	2960	250
.243 WSM	100	3110	300
.25-06 Rem.	120	2990	360
.270 Win.	130	3060	390
.270 Win.	150	2850	295
.270 WSM	150	3150	450
7mm-08 Rem.	140	2860	400
7 x 57 Waters	140	2650	300
.280 Rem.	150	2970	435
.280 Rem.	160	2840	500
7mm WSM	150	3200	500
7mm Rem. Mag.	150	3110	485
7mm Rem. Mag.	175	2860	575
7mm Rem. SA/UM	140	3175	500
7mm Rem. UM	140	3425	500
.30-30 Win.	170	2200	140
.308 Win.	150	2820	345
.308 Win.	180	2620	425
.30-06 Sprng.	150	2910	435
.30-06 Sprng.	180	2700	460
.300 WSM	150	3300	500
.300 Rem. SA/UM	150	3200	450
.300 Rem. SA	150	3450	500
.300 Win. Mag.	180	2960	645
.375 Win.	200	2200	175
.444 Marlin	269	2335	250
.450 Hornady	350	2100	250
.45-70 Govt.	300	1880	225

The new in-lines such as the T/C Encore Omega, Knight DISC Rifle, Winchester Muzzleloader, Savage 10 ML, and Remington 700 ML enable the deer hunter to take advantage of special muzzle-loading only deer hunts and, with a little practice, hunt with the same confidence as he does with his center fire rifle.

This is not to say that there is no longer a place for traditional muzzleloading rifles, far from it, but for those who want to take up muzzleloading simply to get in more days afield deer hunting, they should consider the new generation of muzzleloading rifles.

Last year I took a .50 caliber T/C Encore 209 X 50 muzzleloading rifle on a deer hunt on a private farm where the shots could be very long due to the size of the fields where the deer fed. Before the hunt, I began practicing with the rifle at ranges out to 200 yards. I had mounted a T/C 3 X 9 muzzleloading riflescope and was shooting three pellets of Hodgdon Pyrodex powder. I selected a 180-grain Hornady XTP/Mag sabot pistol bullet as the projectile. It took about a week of daily practice but I soon got to where I could shoot a 4-inch group consistently at 150 yards.

Soon I was on the first day of the hunt. I had spent the first morning of the hunt stalk hunting. I must admit that most of the time was really spent scouting. Just before noon I found a small creek that ran along the base of a wooded ridge for about a quarter-mile to a large field planted in winter wheat. The creek was almost hidden by alders which had grown along the banks hiding it from sight if you drove the farm roads. Along the bank of the creek was a heavily used deer trail and the alders were dotted with fresh rubs. I wanted to hunt this hidden corridor.

That afternoon I took a stand on the edge of the alders, near the winter wheat field. I wanted to be able to see into the alders and the edge of the field where the trail ended at the same time. The afternoon passed with no sign of deer. I thought I had made a judgment error as to how much this trail was used. As the sun was sinking, and as I was thinking about the warm fire at the cabin, I caught sight of a deer silently moving along the alders toward the field. I eased my rifle onto my shooting sticks and waited to see if it was a buck. Out of the corner of my eye, I saw a deer already out in the field. "How did it get there without me seeing it?" I thought, as I slowly turned to take a better look. There, already feeding, was a really nice eight-point buck. Using a rangefinder, I read the distance at 179 yards.

I doubted whether I could make the shot with the Encore but it had shot so well at 150 yards I decided to give it a try. Besides, it was getting dark. I slowly set up for the shot. The buck was broadside to me and feeding. I held the reticle centered just under the buck's spine and slowly squeezed the trigger. White smoke filled the air at the report and I heard the bullet strike. As the smoke cleared, I used my binocular to confirm the buck was down for the count. It was a shot I would never have even thought about with a traditional muzzleloading rifle.

West

Quite a few years ago I interviewed an old Texas sheriff about a monstrous whitetail he had taken many years earlier. He had shot the buck while tracking an escaped prisoner through the dense blackbrush, granjeno, nopal thorn, and spine-infested thickets of Maverick County, only a few miles north of the Rio Grande. The old sheriff knew he was getting close to the capture based on the fresh brogan tracks in last night's rain-soaked South Texas mud. His mind on the prisoner, suddenly before him stood the biggest whitetail buck he had seen in a lifetime of hunting some of the best ranches on both sides of the Rio in the famed Brush Country. Never before had he seen such a sizable rack, nor one with more mass. For the moment he totally forgot about the prisoner. In the saddle scabbard on the horse he was leading was a Model 95 Winchester in .30-06. But the deer was so close that there would not be time to grab the rifle. Without further thinking he drew the holstered .44 Colt Peacemaker he carried cross-draw fashion on his left side. In one swift motion he drew the revolver, thumbed back the hammer, aimed, and shot the buck just below his chin. The deer collapsed. As soon as he had fired the shot he remembered the escaped prisoner he was tracking.

Immediately he hollered out "Billy Boy, you better get here quick or the next one's gonna be for you!"

Mere moments later the escapee came trotting out of the brush with his hands held high to surrender to the fast-thinking sheriff. Before putting cuffs on the prisoner the successful hunter/law enforcer made him load the big buck onto his saddle for the trip back to the nearest ranch house.

Having long been a handgun hunting fan I asked the sheriff why he shot the big buck with the old Peacemaker. His steely gray eyes looked right at me as he spoke in a loud voice, "Heck son, there wasn't time for anything else and at the moment that sidearm was the only gun I had available!"

Unlike that western sheriff, today we have a tremendous number of guns available to us, including rifles and handguns of various designs and descriptions, as well as a variety of muzzleloaders and shotguns. And for those who prefer to hunt with stick and strings, the bows and arrows have never in history been better.

I do not hunt with bow and arrow. I have in the past and have taken numerous whitetails with archery equipment. Over the years as a gun writer I made the decision to only hunt with firearms! I've come to believe the sweetest perfume in the world is the aroma of very recently ignited gunpowder sending a speeding bullet at a whitetail or other big game animal! Thus my discussion here will not include bows and arrows.

Choosing the ideal western firearm requires a bit of knowledge about ballistics, accuracy, downrange energy and terminal bullet performance. As to which guns are ideal, I have my opinions and those may or may not agree with the opinions of others.

As a research biologist numerous years ago with Texas' Wildlife Disease Project, it fell upon me to be one of the primary "collectors" of whitetails and other Texas game animals for most all of the research being conducted at that time. During those years I shot whitetails with everything from .17 calibers to .45 calibers. I used a wide variety of bullet designs and performed complete necropsies (animal term for autopsies) on every critter taken, among other reasons to determine the effects of shot placement and terminal bullet performance. Wish I could have had access back then to some of the calibers and bullets we today have available to us. It would have been interesting.

Hunting western whitetail habitats, shots at deer tend to be long. But, they can also sometimes be extremely close such as when hunting dense thickets, narrow creek bottoms, or when rattling. There are those who would recommend using different guns for each of those circumstances, but I am not one of those.

For years as a gun writer, particularly while with *Shooting*

Larry Weishuhn (left) congratulates Wayne Fears on dropping this southeastern 6-pointer with a 7mm JDJ Contender fired from his T/C Encore.

Times magazine, every time I went to the field I did so with a different gun. Very seldom did I get to use the same gun more than once. At first this was a lot of fun, but then my opinions about constantly changing guns changed and over time I have become a firm believer in pretty well using the same rifle for all my deer hunting. My choices of calibers and firearms? I much prefer hunting with single-shot rifles and handguns. My favorite is the Thompson/Center Encore, both rifle and pistol, chambered in .30-06 Springfield, but more about them later.

Much of the West can be hunted with rifle, handgun, and muzzleloader. Some of the western states, such as Iowa which lies just west of the Mississippi, essentially our dividing line between East and West, allow those with a deer license to hunt with either shotgun or muzzleloader, and muzzleloaders can be used even during the shotgun sea-

son. While there have been huge advances in shotguns especially in terms of rifled barrels and more accurate and harder hitting slugs, for the life of me I cannot understand why anyone would use a shotgun, when they could be using a muzzleloader. Muzzleloaders, especially in-lines, have considerably more accurate longer range capabilities. They are certainly no more difficult to shoot. For that reason I will not discuss shotguns as potential western deer guns.

RIFLE AND HANDGUN CALIBERS

In his portion of this chapter Fears discussed the necessity of understanding downrange energy. For the most part I thoroughly agree with his statement that a cartridge must produce and maintain a minimum of 1200 foot-pounds of energy to be considered worthy of being called a deer cartridge. I further agree that at whatever range the energy level falls below that 1200 foot-pounds of energy, it ceases to be considered a deer cartridge and shots beyond whatever that distance is should not be taken by the hunter. He enumerates several cartridges and distances at which the energy level drops beyond our accepted figure.

Where there is a bit of room for argument comes in terms of some of the revolver handgun cartridges used by deer hunters these days.

HANDGUNS

Before getting into a discussion of handgun calibers let me state up-front I am not a fan of semi-autos when it comes to hunting. For me, hunting handguns include only revolvers and single-shots. I am also not a fan of the .357 Magnum when it comes to hunting deer; in my opinion it should not be used, but there are numerous very dedicated and serious whitetail handgun hunters who have used the cartridge with great success. For the most part, however, those particular hunters are expert shots and they do not shoot unless the range is close, 50 yards or less, and shot placement through the ribcage can be precisely made.

Stepping up, I have shot a number of deer with the .44 Magnum, .454 Casull, and a couple with the .480 Ruger. The .454 Casull is by far the most powerful of these and with most loads retains more energy at 100 yards (generally in excess of 1200 foot-pounds of energy, depending upon bullet and load) than the .44 Magnum produces at the muzzle (approximately 700 to 800 foot-pounds of energy, depending upon bullet and load). The .480 Ruger depending upon of the load and bullet will generally retain about 1100 foot-pounds of energy out to 100 yards. In my opinion all three of these are good whitetail handgun calibers. I own and have hunted with several revolvers chambered for these three cartridges, including those produced by Freedom Arms, Taurus, Ruger, and Colt.

Using the excellent Winchester Partition Gold and Hornady's JHP/XTP and XTP-Mag bullets and loads I have

Potent short and fat cartridges for short actions and handguns are making their appearances in western hunting camps.

taken numerous big bodied whitetails out to my self-imposed distance of 75 yards. I know these calibers with good bullets and loads could kill a western whitetail at a greater distance, but I limited myself to shots within that distance. Out to 75 yards I feel confident of making the shot and placing it where it should go. Remember part of the fun of hunting with a revolver is in getting close.

In terms of sights on revolvers, my preference is using low variable power scopes, those in or approaching the 1.5 to 4X range. These allow for quick pointing and target lock-on. Because of diminishing eyesight I seldom shoot open-sight revolvers because of my difficulty of seeing "open" sights. Red dot sights excite some and they have value in certain handgun hunting situations, but for whatever reason, most of my hunting revolvers are topped with low magnification variables.

My favorite hunting handguns are the single shots, as I have already mentioned, the T/C Encore, T/C Contender, and the T/C G2 Contender. I have taken some of my best western whitetails with the Encore and various Contenders.

I am a firm believer in using enough gun to get the job done! That means delivering sufficient down-range energy out to 300 or more yards, accurate and precise bullet placement using a sufficiently large caliber.

Since 1995, when it was introduced, most of my handgun hunting has been done with a 15-inch barrel T/C Encore handgun chambered for .30-06 Springfield. I've used that particular Encore not only in Texas, but in several other states where deer hunting with such handguns is legal. Not only has it helped me account for a considerable number of big whitetails, I've used the same handgun on moose, caribou, elk, pronghorn, and other big game, including a hunt in South Africa. My .30-06 Encore is one in which I have great faith. I know the gun's capabilities and my capabilities with it. I know that Encore handgun will do its part if I do mine. With a wide variety of factory ammunition shooting

Larry Weishuhn prefers this T/C Encore rifle due to the ability to quickly change barrels.

Bolt-action rifles, like this Browning A-Bolt Stalker, remain the most common choice for western hunters.

150, 165, and 180 grain bullets of most makes, it consistently shoots 1-inch or less groups from the bench at 100 yards. That particular Encore handgun has been topped with a 2.5-7X T/C variable scope since the day it arrived. But only seldom has the magnification ring been turned any higher than 5X.

During a recent deer hunt with worldwide handgun hunter Mark Hampton we discussed our favorite handgun deer-hunting cartridges. Mark's favorite is the .308 Winchester also chambered in the T/C Encore handgun. Although he has used a variety of guns on his hunts, this is the gun he returns to again and again. He knows when the moment of truth arrives, the T/C Encore is not going to let him down.

The T/C Encore features interchangeable barrels which are available in a wide variety of calibers including .270 Winchester and 7mm-08 Remington. Both are equally good deer calibers.

The T/C Contender and the more recently released T/C G2 Contender also have interchangeable barrels but are not designed to handle the pressures produced by the sharp shouldered cartridges that can be chambered in the Encore model.

For years I hunted with a T/C Contender in .30-30 Winchester. I was introduced to some of the wildcat cartridges designed by J. D. Jones of SSK Industries by none other than J. Wayne Fears, the first time he came to hunt whitetails with me. Wayne let me shoot a 7 JDJ Contender. I was hooked and shortly thereafter I was shooting a .309 JDJ Contender that, until the introduction of the Encore, was my absolute favorite handgun.

Handgun hunting for whitetails is a genuine blast. Give me my .30-06 Encore handgun and I'm happy.

One thing I have learned over the years of hunting with handguns — the same thing holds true for rifles — a solid rest when shooting at game is imperative. I used to say I spent half my time looking for game and the other half looking for a solid rest. Now, with my Stoney Point shooting sticks at hand, I can devote full time looking for deer.

RIFLES

For years some of the more popular western whitetail cartridges have been the .270 Winchester, .308 Winchester, and .30-06 Springfield with the bolt action being the most popular type of action. I suspect that is still the case. The late 1900s saw a shift toward more .300 Winchester Magnums, 7mm Remingtons, and 7mm STWs. I suspect in time more and more .270 and .300 Winchester Short Magnums

A hunter takes careful aim over a pile of rails with a Knight Master Hunter muzzleloader. In the West, special muzzle-loading seasons often fall during the best times to hunt mature whitetail bucks.

as well as a few of Remington's versions of those same, short and fat rounds will make their appearances in western whitetail camps.

My favorite deer cartridges for years have been the .270 Winchester, .280 Remington, .30-06 Springfield, and .300 Winchester Magnum. Not only are these flat shooting and hard hitting rounds, but you can walk into practically any sporting goods dealer or even a convenience store throughout the West that sells ammunition and find ammo for these rounds. These are favorite rounds shared by a tremendous number of western deer hunters. All four cartridges maintain 1200 foot-pounds of energy out to 400 yards and beyond with any factory load.

My rifles chambered for these rounds are sighted in to shoot approximately $1^{1}/_{2}$-inch high at 100 yards, based on ballistics charts and years of experience at the range and in the field shooting I know where the bullet should strike the target at varying yardages out to 400.

Hunting in western habitats, variable scopes work extremely nicely because of the potential of long-range shots. My rifles are topped with variables, in the 3 to 10x range with 38 to 40 mm front objectives and are the best I can find. Like my binoculars they are made by Swarovski Optiks. True, Swarovski optics are expensive, but they're good. The last thing

I want to be concerned about just before I pull the trigger at a distant trophy whitetail is whether or not my scope is going to do what I am about to ask of it.

Your choice of caliber as long as it will produce sufficient downrange energy and deliver pinpoint accuracy is totally up to you. As mentioned we all have favorites. The same is true for actions.

Most western deer hunters use bolt-action rifles produced by Browning, Remington, Ruger, Sako, U.S.R.A.C. (Winchester), and others, including numerous custom rifle makers. A good bolt-action rifle tends to be accurate, fast handling, safe, and can provide a quick second shot if needed.

While bolt-action rifles are the most popular type of action used by western deer hunters, there is a growing number of serious whitetail hunters who are now using single-shots, specifically Ruger Number 1s, Mossberg SSI One, H&R, the T/C Encore, and T/C G2 Contender Rifle. These single-shots are accurate and fast handling because without the bolt assembly their overall length is shorter. To many hunters, using single-shot rifles denotes a quality experience. I've already stated my preference for hunting with single-shots and specifically the T/C Encore rifle chambered .30-06. The beauty of the Encore is I can quickly change out barrels and turn my rifle into a 12- or 20-gauge shotgun, or if hunting dangerous game to a .375 H&H rifle, or for that matter I can also turn it into a .45 or .50 caliber in-line muzzleloader.

This versatility greatly increases the value of the Encore and a deer hunting rifle, shotgun, and muzzleloader. In switching barrel the butt stock and the trigger always stay the same. Even if you switch barrels you are essentially shooting the same gun all the time!

MUZZLELOADERS

When Tony Knight introduced the world to his in-line .50 caliber MK-85 back in 1985 he revolutionized the world of muzzleloading and muzzleloader hunting. Up to that point flintlocks and cap locks were the norm and were hunted with primarily back East and out West by modern-day "Buckskinners."

It didn't take long for other companies to start producing in-lines as well. Soon muzzleloader seasons were added, and special muzzleloader seasons now occur in several western states and Canadian Provinces. These seasons often fall during ideal times to hunt big mature bucks.

The two most popular muzzleloader calibers for western whitetails are the .45 and the .50, and, where legal, using sabot bullets and propellants such as Hodgdon's Pyrodex and 777. Both propellants are available in loose or pellet forms.

Using magnum loads — 150 grains of Pyrodex or 777, loose or pellet and propelling sabot bullets such as the T/C .50 Shock Wave sabot in 250- or 300-grain — the bullets will retain an excess of 1400 foot-pounds of

Today's muzzleloading bullets can retain 1400 ft.-lbs. of energy at 250 yards.

energy at 250 yards!

There are many fine muzzleloaders that I have used since about 1986 after procuring my first in-line, one of Tony Knight's MK-85s. Knight continues to build extremely good and accurate muzzleloading rifles. CVA is also still in the picture as is Traditions. Both build economical in-line hunting muzzleloaders.

The Thompson/Center Encore rifle can be converted by changing barrels into either a .45 or .50 caliber muzzleloader, known respectively as the 209 x .45 Mag or the 209 x .50 Mag. Both use 209 shotgun primers to ignite the propellant.

I have taken numerous whitetails with both Knight and T/C guns. My favorite two muzzleloaders are the T/C Encore 209 x 50 and the T/C Omega. The T/C Omega has a 28-inch barrel that uses a full 150 grains of propellant, but because of its simple sealed pivoting breech the overall length is, in some instances, shorter than other .50 caliber muzzleloaders with shorter barrels.

With modern muzzleloaders, specially designed bullets, and modern black powder substitutes, it is not uncommon to shoot groups of $1^1/2$ inches or less at 100 yards. With a solid rest this makes these same muzzleloaders effective on whitetails at 200 or more yards. In addition, thanks to technology, cleaning a muzzleloader is no longer a mess or a problem.

Remember, laws and regulations regarding muzzleloaders, rifles, shotguns, and handguns continually change. Before going to the field always be certain of the specific rules and regulations in the area you choose to hunt.

We have many choices with which to hunt our favorite game animal. Choosing the ideal firearm comes down to personal preferences and spending time at the range getting to know how and where it shoots at varying distances. Regardless of which firearm you choose, remember to practice, practice, and then practice some more. When that western buck of a lifetime is standing out there at 320 yards, you'll be ready for him.

Scouting East & West

Finding fresh and active buck rubs, particularly rubs on larger trees like the oak shown here, are prime indications that you are in a buck's territory.

East

I remember as a teenager following an old master deer hunter around hoping to pick up his deer hunting tricks. As we would walk across the hills, he would read deer signs like a scholar reads a book. Every track, trail, rub, and dropping gave him a hint as to how to properly plan his hunt. After several of these scouting trips the old hunter would get a twinkle in his eye and tell me that he knew where he was going to kill his buck. Sure enough, each year he scored and usually in the area we scouted.

PRESEASON SCOUTING

Scouting a month or more before deer season opens is good for learning the terrain; however, your more serious scouting should take place as near the season as possible. Eastern deer habits have a way of changing just as hunting season opens. They begin switching from late summer foods to fall foods. Colder days mean that bedding areas will change. The rut is coming on and the bucks are becoming restless. The later you scout, the more accurate and up-to-date your finds will be and you stand better odds of being at the right place at the right time on opening morning.

As you scout your deer hunting area looking for signs, it is advisable to carry a U.S.G.S. topo map or aerial photo with you. Using a topo map or aerial photo to record your findings on gives you an excellent "memory bank" to use for planning hunts. By marking trails, bedding areas, feeding areas, and scrapes on the map you will see a system appear before your eyes. This map will tell you where to locate your stand, or where best to stalk. Topo maps and aerial photos can be downloaded by going to website: www. terraserver.microsoft.com.

There have been many magazine articles and books written on what to look for when scouting so we won't go into the details of basic signs in this book. However, we will give you some pointers so the signs will not mislead you.

Deer Droppings: One of the signs that mislead many beginning hunters are deer droppings. To the novice, deer droppings mean "deer are here!" This may or may not be true. Let's look at a few facts. Deer droppings come in two basic shapes—round and oblong. At first glance they look like rabbit droppings; however, rabbit droppings are smaller and are much more fibrous than those of the deer. Fresh deer droppings are shiny black and are moist for the first day. Older droppings have a dry and dull appearance. Fresh deer droppings are a sign that deer are using the area. However, don't get excited and think that when you find several piles of deer droppings that the area contains a lot of deer. Wildlife researchers have found that a deer may deposit droppings up to 12 times a day.

Deer Tracks: The deer sign that has more myth associated with it than any other of the signs is the track. Many hunters think that all tracks are fresh; others think that deer tracks always lead to a deer; while others claim to distinguish a buck track from a doe track. In many cases, none of these are true. Deer tracks generally tell you one thing — deer have been there. Do not be misled by numbers of tracks as one deer can make a lot of tracks. Do not waste your time trying to distinguish buck tracks from doe tracks. Contrary to the opinion of many hunters, there is usually little difference. In the far north, some hunters can distinguish a buck track in the snow after studying the trail for a distance, but this is the exception. Large tracks, or tracks showing the dew claws, may be made just as much by a running doe or a heavy doe as by a buck. While tracks are an important sign, they are limited as to what they tell you.

Feeding Areas: Deer food in the East may not be considered a deer sign by many hunters; however, I think it should be treated as a sign when scouting. When scouting for deer signs watch for preferred deer food such as white oak acorns, Japanese honeysuckle, greenbrier (smilax), or a field of soybeans, wheat, or oats. These foods attract deer. When you find a deer food area look for fresh

tracks and fresh droppings. If you find these signs together, you may have found a place for a stand. Mark the food area on your topo map for future reference. Also, look for deer trails leading into the food area and mark these trails on your map. These trails make good stand sites.

Bedding Areas: Deer beds are a difficult sign to find and to read when found. Wildlife researchers have found that bed locations vary considerably with individual deer and are distributed widely throughout the home range of the individual deer. In addition, bedding sites vary by habitat differences. On a cold, sunny day deer like to bed down in the warm sun in a dry place such as in a broom sedge field. During periods of bad weather, such as cold, rainy, windy days, they like to bed in dense evergreens, protected from the elements. Once hunting pressure is on, you will find beds in the edge of thick brush where the deer can see danger coming. One jump will usually assure them a safe exit. Preferred bedding sites can vary widely from deer found in Michigan cedar swamps to deer found in Virginia mountains to deer found in flat southern pine forest. The one thing that is common with all sites is that bucks like the thickest sites they can find.

Deer Trails: A sight that excites most deer hunters is a well-worn trail or runway, as some hunters prefer to call them. Eastern deer trails are best described as paths of least resistance followed by deer, bucks going around obstructions and, if possible, does going under them whenever encountered. Some are as long as a mile; others

are as short as a few yards across a stream or saddle between two hills. Some are used for only a month or so and others are known to exist for years. Generally speaking, the most common deer trail found is one that begins as several faint trails, leading from bedding areas, which come together to form a more prominent trail that leads to a favored feeding area. As long as the food in the feeding area is available, the trail will be active. When the food supply is exhausted, the trail may be abandoned.

There are many animals that make trails, so the deer hunter will do well to scout a newfound trail for fresh deer droppings and deer tracks. One fall, I was hunting with a youngster in West Virginia on his first deer hunt. The second morning, he came rushing into camp exclaiming that he had found a heavily used deer trail leading from a wooded ridge down to a small lake. I got my bow and followed him back to the trail. Indeed, it was being used, but not by deer. My young friend had found a trail made by beavers dragging saplings and small logs into the lake. Confirm your trail. Make sure that you are spending your days watching deer trails and not beaver, cow, or fox trails.

The hunter who finds a good deer trail should mark the trail on his topo map. More than likely it will join up a bedding area or feeding area you have already marked. If not, it may lead to such areas.

Rubs and Scrapes: Perhaps the best signs to the buck hunter are fresh rubs and scrapes. One buck may make many rubs. I like to find rubs when scouting because it means I am in a buck's territory. I especially like to find large trees, eight inches or larger in diameter, rubbed as this is usually done by larger bucks.

Scrapes are a better sign to find as bucks often return to scrapes to freshen up the scent he has left there as a part of the mating cycle. Active scrapes can be a good place to take a stand.

Through preseason scouting can be some of the most valuable time you can spend in preparation for the hunt. Learning to read signs and keeping a detail record of your findings will generally spell the difference between success and failure during the coming deer season.

As I learned from the old hunter, preseason scouting is not a deep, dark secret. It is simply knowing what to look for and the ability to put the signs together to plan a successful hunt. By using a topo map as an aid, you too can put the clues together to solve the mystery of where old mossy horns can be found.

ARMCHAIR SCOUTING

This was the worst whitetail hunt I had been on in a long time. A friend had given me permission to hunt his 1200-acre farm that was located in the southern part of Mississippi. Because I had been on a number of back-to-back hunts, I did not have the opportunity to drive down to the farm and scout the property.

On the opening morning of deer season, I had driven three hours to be on the farm at daybreak. I easily found the front gate of the farm. As dawn was breaking in the east, I left my truck and started walking toward the north. The landowner had told me there was a creek up that way with a lot of acorn-bearing oaks growing along the bank where the deer fed every morning.

In the dim light, I made my way north. As I walked, the vegetation became thicker, and soon I was barely able to move through the thick tangle of cane and greenbrier. It was obvious I was in a thick

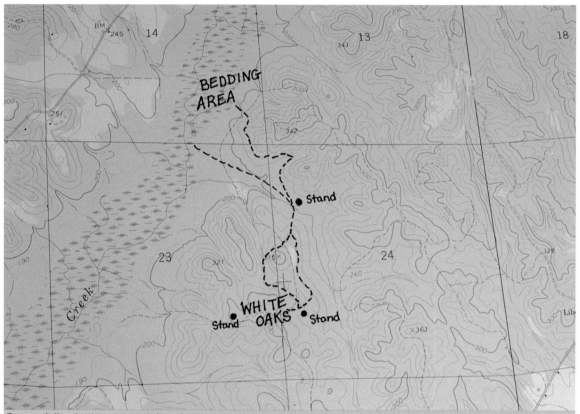

By carefully plotting out scouting clues on a good topographical map, a hunter can find the pattern that helps tag that elusive trophy buck. To obtain a detailed U.S.G.S. topographical map of your hunhting area, access: http://stoegerbooks.mapcard.com.

creek bottom swamp without an oak in sight.

It was long after sunup when I reached the creek, which more properly should have been called a river. My clothing was torn from the walk through the briers, and I was soaked with perspiration. I found a few small oaks but no acorn-bearing trees. To make matters worse, the swamp was so thick I could not see 20 yards in any direction. I decided to sit down and catch my breath before walking back through the jungle.

As I sat cursing my bad luck, I heard barking dogs running in my direction. Soon the swamp was filled with the howling of a large number of hounds. Obviously, someone was conducting a deer drive nearby. My so-called stalk hunt was ruined.

What went wrong with this hunt? If I had had time to scout the property, I could have avoided many of the problems. However, even without on-site scouting, my situation could have been improved had I taken the time to exercise a strategy for learning new land that many experienced hunters call "armchair scouting."

Even if you scout out a tract of land in person, you would be wise to talk to those who visit or travel near the property regularly. In the East the deer population density is greater than in the West, and deer territories are much smaller. By interviewing those who live or travel near the property you can learn much about the patterns of the deer.

If, in today's fast-paced world, hunters learn of new hunting grounds but do not have the time for preseason scouting, they can put armchair scouting to work. It can be a fun-filled adventure in itself, like solving a mystery. Here is how to go about it.

Obtain a U.S. Geological Survey topographical map or aerial photo of the area. Once you have a topo map and/or an aerial photo of your hunting property, you are ready to get more current information. You can do this by telephone.

Begin by calling the landowner or his agent, such as a farm manager, managing forester, or land manager. Since this person is on the land regularly, he can possess a wealth of information about the property. Ask questions such as: Are the boundary lines marked? You do not want to get onto another person's property. Does anyone else have hunting rights on the property? It could be that you are sharing the area with many more hunters. How do the deer

A hunter examines deer droppings at the margin of a crop field. Droppings, combined with other sign, can provide some idea as to what the deer are doing.

hunters in the area hunt? Remember the experience I had with the deer-hunting dogs. What land management practices are planned for the next few months? You do not want to plan a hunt along a ridge that is going to be clear-cut the week before the season opens. It would, however, be great to learn that a field is planted in alfalfa that should be about four inches high on opening weekend. Where has the owner/manager been seeing most the bucks? I leaned the locations of some of the best bucks I have taken simply by asking someone who worked on the property.

Be sure to have your topo map and/or aerial photograph in front of you as you interview this person. It will make understanding his directions much easier. If he talks about a deer trail leading from his apple orchard across a creek and onto a ridge running parallel to the railroad, you can see it all in front of you and even mark it for future reference.

Next, call the county Agricultural Extension Service agent in the county where the property is located. He is familiar with the entire county and can give you valuable information on the local deer population, what crops the deer are feeding on, hunting techniques used by hunters in the area, local butcher and freezer information, and often current deer information on the property itself. Once a county agent saved me a lot of time by telling me there was a new landfill adjacent to the property where I planned to hunt, and the landfill had attracted a large number of feral dogs that had chased the deer off the property.

One of the most valuable calls you can make is to the state Department of Natural Resources wildlife biologist who works in the area. He can give you approximate rutting dates, deer population estimates, foods the deer favor, local problems you might encounter such as heavy poaching, problems with conflicting hunting interests, land management problems such as a recent clear-cut, late fall prescribed forest burning, etc. Many times the biologist can suggest hunting techniques and strategies that are unique to that area. The same thing is true if you place a call to the local conservation officer. He knows the local area well and is up-to-date on the deer situation in your area of interest.

One word of caution: These people are busy and cannot sit around listening to all your deer hunting stories. When you call any of these officials, be well organized and have your questions written down. Be courteous, and do not waste his time. I have usually found these people willing to share helpful information with the caller who is well organized and gets to the points quickly.

Be creative in your research. One year when I was in college and did not have the time or financial resources to physically scout a small farm, I tried to call the landowner and officials listed above. Due to meetings, sick leave, etc., I could not find anyone to talk with. Out of desperation, I called the rural mail carrier who drove daily on roads that passed on two sides of the farm. It turned out he was a hunter who told me about a nine-pointer he saw on a regular basis. As he described the area over the phone, I marked the road crossing on my topo map. That Thanksgiving I found the trails the buck used at the road crossing just as the mail carrier

Ben Lee (left), Wayne Fears (center), and Fred Bear (right) examine a rub during the early part of the bow season.

described, and I took the buck the second morning.

This is not in any way to imply you should not spend time on a new hunting property scouting for sign and getting to know the lay of the land. However, in those cases where an actual visit to the property is impossible, do not give up scouting. Simply purchase a topo map and aerial photo, study them, and put in some time on the phone putting the clues together that will solve the mystery of where you can find a buck. More often than not, the information you compile will put you on the property knowing it almost as well as if you scouted it in person.

POSTSEASON SCOUTING CAN BE VERY REVEALING

Many years ago when I first started guiding hunters on spring gobbler hunts, I made it a point to start my scouting as soon as the deer season was over. The month of February and the first half of March found me in the woods looking for turkey sign and watching turkeys. The very first year I started this early intensive turkey-scouting program, I noticed something that caught me by surprise. While looking for turkey sign, I was finding an enormous amount of fresh deer sign. I was finding the hidden areas where big bucks spend the winter after the pressure of hunting season had pushed them into deep hiding.

I found 2-month-old rubs and scrapes in areas that had been totally overlooked by hunters. In March, I found shed antlers and saw signs of heavy feeding on

Active scrapes can be a good place to look for a stand location.

smilax and honeysuckle. Early that spring I jumped bucks that still had their racks, in areas so difficult to get to that I hadn't bothered to hunt there that fall.

This discovery of buck wintering grounds sparked an idea that was to be a great hunting aid the next season. Throughout the entire turkey-scouting period and turkey season, I kept a set of notes on my findings and sightings. By April, I had located several pockets of land that obviously had been retreats where bucks spent the winter. It was my plan to go into these areas late in the next deer season and do some intensive hunting.

The next fall I waited until midway through the deer season and started hunting my newfound areas. The results were three nice bucks. When I was asked by my friends how I had found these deer, my answer was "postseason scouting." You can bet I got some strange looks.

In order to understand why

postseason scouting is valuable, one must first understand what is happening. In many states, such as Alabama and South Carolina, the deer seasons are long, and even in states or areas where the deer season is shorter, a lot of hunting pressure is brought to bear on the bucks. Big bucks react to this pressure by reducing their daylight activity until most become nocturnal. As the pressure continues and these night-traveling bucks are jumped from their hiding areas by roaming hunters, they begin to seek areas where human pressure is less.

At the same time that hunting pressure is causing mature bucks to move to new locations within their territory, a natural occurrence is adding pressure. Late in the year, the fall food crop gets scarcer, especially during years of poor mast production. The fall crop of acorns and other nuts, soft mast, corn, soybeans, and a lot of the green browse play out late in the deer season. The green understory vegetation which has provided a lot of cover is disappearing.

These two factors combined cause the bucks to change their diets and to seek more cover. This usually means a move to areas that are thick and contain food such as smilax, honeysuckle, mushrooms, and low-growing twigs. In many cases, this is a move into moist, low areas with rich soil, such as beaver swamps, creek bottoms, and along rivers. In some cases, this can be a move to thick fencerows or wood lots adjacent to fields planted in winter pasture crops such as wheat, oats, or rye. The bucks lay up in

People who frequent your hunting territory, such as rural mail carriers, can give you important information about buck movements and location.

the thick areas during the day and feed in the adjacent fields at night.

I have seen bucks move into an area of young, thickly planted pines during this period. They move out of the pines at night but hold up tight in them during the day. In addition, I have seen them move into a thick pocket of vegetation in the middle of a clear-cut.

I do not want to sound like bucks in the East go great distances to seek new hideouts during the winter, for this is not necessarily so. They simply seek out the overlooked corners and pockets of habitat that is in or near their territory where cover is abundant and food is nearby. They stay in these wintering areas until the hunting pressure is gone and spring brings out an abundance of food throughout their territory. Then they move out to roam their home range.

Postseason scouting should begin as soon as the deer season ends. The first step is to try to find the overlooked habitat that the big bucks may have retreated to. More often than not, it will be an area that is extremely thick with understory vegetation. This may be a creek bottom that is thick with cane, vines, etc. It could be an area in an old stand of planted pines where the blackberry vines are so thick that it has kept hunters out. An island thick with cover in a river or swamp can often hold a buck or two.

In many situations, the cover doesn't have to be so thick. More open woods near buildings or in areas that are not hunted can be good wintering grounds. Many years ago when I worked on the Swannoochee Wildlife Management Area in south Georgia one of the largest bucks on the area spent the hunting season around the check station where there was no

hunting. When I owned Stagshead Hunting Lodge in Alabama, we had a huge buck that spent the hunting season around the shooting range. There was a lot of shooting but no hunting pressure.

At another hunting lodge I once owned, a road makes a loop around several thousand acres of wet flatwoods. It is a mile from one side of the loop to the other. One year while postseason scouting, I found a pocket of relatively open woods in the center, which was the winter home for these big bucks. Hunters, during deer season, had only hunted the first one-quarter mile of woods off the loop road. The center of the loop was wet and muddy. No one bothered to go into the center. Since there was plenty of browse in that area, the bucks were living "the good life" without being bothered by man.

To find areas such as this, try to put yourself in the place of the bucks. Where would you go to be safe and yet be close to food? Answer that question and do your postseason scouting there.

Signs to look for during this period are similar to signs you would look for during a preseason scouting trip with an exception or two. Since the bucks — and often retreating does as well — are confined to a smaller area with thick vegetation, they will create more visible trails than they normally would. Often by following these trails, I have found the main wintering ground. While in most cases the rut will be over, be observant for rubs and scrapes.

One sign I look hard for in the spring are dropped antlers. It is a sure sign that you are in a buck's home. I mark it on a topo map for future reference. Usually I find only one antler since the buck rarely sheds both at the same time or in the same place.

If you hunt several areas, you would be wise to mark the postseason sign you find on a topo map. After several seasons of scouting, these records will become valuable when you are planning a mid- to late season hunt.

Once you have found a lot of postseason sign and may have possibly seen bucks during your scouting trips, your work is complete until the next deer season. When the season opens you can hunt the areas you regularly hunt. Save the wintering grounds for the last part of the season when the hunting pressure in on. The hunter who knows where the big bucks spend the winter knows the best places to hunt during the latter part of the next season.

West

f you had seen my two daughters and me running through the woods, converging toward a spot on the ground some 30 yards away, you might have thought we had just spotted a five-dollar gold piece and were running to be the first to claim it. Theresa, my older daughter, was in the lead for a short while. I was gaining and just when victory was in sight, Beth, the younger daughter, ran between us and claimed the prize.

What was it? Why a matched set of shed antlers from a four-year-old typical twelve-pointer that we had seen a few times before deer season had opened three months earlier. That had been the last time he had been seen. Throughout the six-week-long Texas whitetail season neither we, nor any of the other hunters on the property, had seen that buck. I had been concerned that he might have died, but here was proof that he had indeed survived the season. Chances appeared excellent he would produce even bigger antlers the coming fall. Before the afternoon's shed hunt was over we had collected no less than 20 recently cast antlers which provided considerable information about the sizes, ages, and whereabouts of particular bucks.

The early spring Saturday afternoon antler hunt had become a weekend ritual. Both daughters, then ages 12 and 10, loved spending time on the ranches I managed, and thoroughly enjoyed shed hunting. It was sort of like searching for Easter eggs, only more exciting. To them and me it was great fun spending time together engaged in friendly competition to see which of us could find more cast antlers, while gathering considerable data about the local deer herd and particular bucks.

SCOUTING DATA

Quite a few years ago I started recording information about the different ranches I managed and hunted in spiral and loose-leaf notebooks. Generally, my first step was to procure a map of the property, either a topographical map from the U.S. Geological Survey, or an aerial photo from the Soil Conservation Service —now called the U.S. Natural Resource Conservation Service. If a no quality map was available I hand-drew a map of the property with all the pertinent landmarks. Occasionally, even if there was an aerial map, I still hand-drew an enlarged section of certain parts of the property.

On the map I recorded as much deer sign information as possible, with special notes within the body of the notebook about what was seen, what was found, where and when.

Information that was marked on the map included concentrations of particular types of vegetation, water sources, trails, location of shed antlers, rubs, scrapes, unused deer stands, suspected bedding areas, current feeding areas, and deer sightings.

Not only did the notebooks and maps serve as storage for scouting reports, they also recorded patterns to help in interpreting the information collected.

WHEN TO SCOUT

I do most of my on-site scouting in western deer habitat beginning a couple of weeks after the season closes. By then the deer have started to settle down and have returned to their natural patterns.

During the late winter, if there is not a tremendous amount of snow on the ground, you can still see where bucks had established scrapes. Even with snow on the ground you can still determine where scrapes were by looking for overhanging branches that were "nuzzled" by bucks. Rubs are visible at this time and show recent use. Trails are obvious, and there is a good chance you might catch glimpses of bucks. Depending upon where you scout, you might also start finding some cast antlers.

Postseason scouting gives you a pretty good idea of what is left after the season closes, does not overly upset the deer, and will give you a pretty good idea where to start hunting when next fall's season rolls around.

With mature bucks, if you put too much pressure on them, especially right before the season opens you can cause them to completely change their normal habits, including going totally nocturnal. That is why I try to do much of my scouting postseason. During late summer and early fall most of my scouting is done from "afar" with binoculars, or simply spot-checking to be certain food sources haven't changed, water holes haven't dried up and there haven't been any other major changes to the habitat that would cause deer to change their fall habits.

Whitetails throughout most of the West are not migratory, like they can be in the northern portions of the East such as in northern Michigan and possibly elsewhere.

SHED ANTLERS

Throughout the western whitetail deer range, much can be learned from the cast or shed antlers. A lot of critters, such as rats, mice, squirrels, and rabbits chew on cast deer antlers. The sign of their chewing can be seen on the antlers and can be distinguished from other animals chewing on them, by looking at the rather small and chisel-like teeth marks. However, if you find fairly recently cast antlers and they show considerable sign of having been chewed on by a larger animal, such as a cow or a deer, it tells you the area you are in is probably deficient in such minerals as calcium, phosphorous, or trace minerals. If you find such chewed upon sheds, and it is legal to do so in that area, consider setting up some mineral licks. Will they do great wonders for the deer herd and antlers? Simply let me say, it certainly won't hurt!

Finding freshly cast antlers tells you the deer that dropped them made it through the hunting season. It also tells you where that deer was at a certain period of time. Mark where you find sheds on your map.

Interestingly in Mexico, South Texas, eastern Colorado, and Wyoming, as well as in Alberta we have often found sheds and the following season killed the deer which dropped them within

A detailed topographical map is a valuable tool in planning your hunt.

Finding freshly cast antlers tells you that the buck that dropped them made it through the hunting season.

less than a quarter of a mile of where the sheds were found.

In southern Texas I have on several occasions found sheds and then the following fall killed the buck that cast them within less than 100 yards of where they were found. No, those deer weren't behind high fences!

The size of the antler will give you a pretty good clue as to how big and how old the buck that dropped them is. Small antlers generally come from young deer, bigger antlers from "coming" bucks, and big antlers from mature deer. However, you can also be a bit more specific as to the age class of the buck that dropped them.

Yearling deer generally produce no more than little 4 by 4 racks, most are smaller. Thus they are easy to determine. Two- and three-year-olds and most four-year-olds produce bigger racks and may have several points per side, decent main beam lengths, good mass and tine length. To confirm such antlers were cast by that age class of bucks, grasp the antler and turn it upside down, so that you are looking at where the antler was attached to the skull. Compare the rough pedicel attachment area below the burr to the diameter and circumference of the main beam just above the burr. In most two- and three-year-olds

and some four-year-olds the pedicel attachment area and the diameter and circumference of the main beam are nearly the same size.

If the antler is big, again turn it upside down and compare the size of the attachment area to the beam just above the burr. If the buck is in his prime, say from four to seven years of age his shed antler will have a sizable pedicel attachment area and the diameter and circumference of the beam just above the burr will be even bigger.

When the buck starts going downhill because of age (and some bucks as long as they continue on good, daily nutrition may continue producing big antlers until they are 10 or 12 years old or older) he will have a large pedicel attachment area, but the beam just above the burr will not be as large.

What's interesting especially where bucks have a tendency to live to maturity and beyond is to find sheds from the same buck in serial years. Then you can really notice the above and also see how he progresses from year to year. Shed hunting can be great fun and highly rewarding!

TRACKS

During a seminar an attendee asked me if there was a sure way to determine the difference between a buck

Larry Weishuhn examines deer tracks along a trail that leads to an active feeding area.

track and that of a big-footed doe. My reply? "There certainly is! You can always tell if they are still standing in those tracks!" For a second that brought numerous puzzled looks. I then continued that in my opinion sometimes you might be able to tell the difference due to size, bucks being larger, but after years of following around big-footed deer I have yet to determine a sure way by simply looking at tracks. Chances are if you spot a track and there is a smaller track following or walking off to the side, it's a doe.

Several of the biggest bucks I've taken from northern Canada to below the Rio Grande had relatively small feet, especially when compared to some of the tracks I watched does leave.

A single deer can make a huge number of tracks and three can make it look like 30 have been in the area. What I try to determine from looking at tracks is where did they come from and where are they going and if it's worthwhile for me to try to set up an ambush spot near a trail.

Where I do pay particular attention to tracks is when I find a trail where deer have been entering a

food plot or feeding area. Once I find such a trail I back-track the trail to try to find where two or more trails converge. That's where I'll look for tracks that look like they were made by a deer that stood around and waited for other deer to come by on their way to the food source. Find such a set of tracks and it's a pretty good bet it was made by a mature buck. Rather than expose himself to danger in the open field, he'll hang back where the trails come together to check every doe that comes past. He may also feed in the food plot, but chances are he'll do it only after dark.

Near where I find such tracks as mentioned is where I'll set up an ambush point, perhaps a tree stand or quite possibly simply sit in a tree where I can see the area. Tracks as a whole indicate the presence of deer, especially if they appear relatively fresh.

DROPPINGS

Several years ago I was involved in a research project that tried to determine the relative worth of pellet count deer surveys, a system that was once used to get a handle on the local deer population where other census methods were useless. Back then biologists determined the average whitetail dropped 12 pellet groups per day. Thus by counting the number of pellet groups within a given area and dividing by 12 they hoped to determine the local deer density.

My part of the program was to determine the validity of this assumption and also determine where deer generally defecated relative to bedding and feeding areas. The trend among the deer we watched, which were in about a 10-acre enclosure, tended to drop pellets most often shortly after they left their bedding areas. They would stand up after having been bedded for a while, stretch and then drop a pellet group. What this told me was that if one found numerous pellet groups, both fresh and old, in an area, it was likely close to the deer's bedding area. Finding such pellet groupings has often helped me establish where deer bed, if indeed bedding and feeding areas are specially separated.

Interestingly in a fair bit of western deer range, bedding areas and feeding areas can be one and the same, rather than the distinctive separation of the two found in eastern habitats. Quite frankly I do not pay much attention to deer droppings when scouting, other than trying to determine the location of bedding areas.

FEEDING AREAS

Deer foods and feeding areas vary greatly between western whitetail habitats. In the Southwest, most of the low-growing brush and the weeds or forbs that grow between them are at worst at least decent deer foods. A bit farther north and west things really don't change all that much other than these areas may have various varieties of oaks which produce acorns. A bit even farther north and west forbs, some woody browse, limited mast producing trees, and agricultural crops provide the primary food source. That situation extends well into Canada. In the extreme northwestern whitetail range, within the Provincial Forest of Canada limited mast producing trees and woody browses and vines as well as spring and summer forbs provide food for whitetails.

The common food sources that run throughout most of the western whitetail's habitat are agricultural crops such as corn, milo, soybeans, wheat, barley, alfalfa, and other similar row and hay crops. These food sources are often bordered by creek bottoms and drainages, CRP grasslands, plum thickets, cattle pastures, or thickets of various sorts.

If you want to learn some of the primary food sources of deer in the area you hunt, contact your state's local wildlife biologist or game warden. He can generally give you a good idea as to what deer eat and when.

During the hunting season when someone kills a deer, I will often ask to be the one to gut it. There is method in my madness. I always try to evaluate shot placement and terminal bullet performance, for one thing. But the other thing I do is once the rumen has been removed, wearing rubber gloves as one should when gutting deer, I'll make a slit in the rumen to see what the deer has been eating. Usually there are bits and pieces of vegetation large enough to determine what they have been eating. And while I may not be able to identify the plant by name, I can get a pretty good idea of what the deer just ate. It may be from something I've seen while hunting. If the rumen contains an abundance of

Rubs on larger trees can be an indication of big bucks. Larger bucks tend to prefer bigger trees.

a particular plant, I'll know that I want to hunt in the area where such plants are in abundance. Scouting never ends!

SCRAPES

Have you ever watched a buck make or refresh a scrape? It is most interesting the ritual a buck goes through. Generally he approaches it from downwind, where he can scent if another buck has been there. Quite often bucks do to scrapes what male pet dogs do to car tires and corners of their territory. They stake claim to it, but then every other male dog that comes by will attempt to "X-out" the previous "visitor." By approaching downwind the buck can smell if the scrape has been visited by another deer since he was last there.

If indeed it has been visited by another buck, or he feels the urge to refresh the scrape, he approaches the pawed-out area under an overhanging branch and generally "nuzzles" or chews a bit on the overhanging limbs, possibly rubs his forehead on the overhanging branch or carefully tries to rub the area right in front of his eye on the branch. He may also "horn" the overhanging branch a bit. Then standing in the pawed-out area below the branch he will generally paw the ground three to five times with each the left and right foot, seldom more and seldom less. The ground freshly pawed, he will step forward, draw his two hind legs kind of under him and then urinate on his legs so the urine trickles down his legs, over his hocks and tarsal glands. He may also while the urine is trickling down, rub his hocks together. When finished the buck walks away. Sometimes I have also seen bucks defecate in the scrape.

The purpose of the scrape may be in part to mark territory, although whitetails as a group are in the truest meaning of the word not territorial. One or many bucks may use the same scrape.

Scrapes generally are most actively maintained during the tail end of the pre-rut, just before the peak of the breeding season.

Some bucks return many times to the same scrape and others may only visit a particular scrape only one time. Incidentally it's been my experience that whenever you start seeing active scrapes from that point on bucks start responding to rattling horns.

Certain scrapes tend to be actively used only a short period of time while others are actively used fall after fall. The longest I have personally seen a scrape be used year after year is 15 years and counting. Every year I have had access to the property the scrape has been actively used.

In scouting these are the type of scrapes I look for and pay particular attention to. Usually very active scrapes are obvious even during the late winter when I do most of my personal scouting.

Research tells us that most of the scraping activity is done by bucks after dark, as high as 75 percent of all scraping activity takes place under the cover of darkness.

RUBS

Rubs are the surest sign of bucks in an area, outside of finding shed antlers and actually sighting bucks.

I personally look for big rubs when scouting because big bucks tend (although not always) to make big rubs. I also look for rubs on trees which show signs of having been rubbed in the past. It's been my experience that some bucks frequently return to rub on the same trees year after year. Finding a good, recent rub which has been previously rubbed in years past catches my interest, especially if it is on a sizable tree and is made a bit higher from the ground than most.

Rubs, as scrapes, are generally made along travel routes. Thus pay attention to which side of the tree they were made. Then start looking for more rubs on that same side of the tree beyond where you found the first one. These "rub lines" will clue you as to the travel route the buck takes and also the direction he usually travels. Research tells us that many whitetail bucks tend to travel in somewhat of an egg-shaped pattern. Mark the rubs you find on your map of the property to try to determine travel routes of bucks.

By looking at the surface of the rub you can get a pretty good idea about the kind of antler the buck that made it has. If the rub's surface is relatively smooth, chances are good the surface of the buck's antlers, especially close to the base and around the brow tines, is also very smooth. If the surface of the rub exhibits deep gouges, chances are pretty good the buck that made it has antlers that have "kicker" points near the base and around the brow tines.

If there is underbrush on either side of the tree beyond where the rub is being made, look for scarring on the limbs and branches. Finding where antler tine tips scarred them may give you a clue as to how

People who work in a hunting area, such as this cowboy, can give valuable information about a buck's location.

long the buck's tines are and the width of his spread.

When scouting pay attention to rubs, whether you are scouting postseason or making a quick reconnoiter through your hunting area in the fall just to be sure things have not changed.

DISTANT SCOUTING

Not all of us are so fortunate that we live close to where we hunt. This is especially true if we are considering going on an out-of-state whitetail hunt. If you can't spend some time in the area there are ways to scout it just the same, but by long distance.

If possible when hunting a new or distant area I try to procure a topographical map of the area. Then once I get such a map I start calling people in the area, perhaps rural mail carriers or school bus drivers who frequently drive through the reasonably immedi-

ate area I hope to hunt. I'll do my best to learn about the terrain to determine if indeed it is as I have pictured it in my mind based on the topo maps. If possible also contact someone who has previously hunted in the area, but don't always put too much faith in what you hear from fellow hunters. If you called me and asked about a particularly favorite hunting area, I'm probably not going to tell you everything I know.

If you're going to hunt in relatively open country, look for drainages on your map and low saddles on ridges that provide access from one creek bottom to another. Remember also that the biggest bucks in otherwise open prairie country are often found in small coulees and rills quite some distance from denser creek bottom country.

Try as best as you can to learn

about the lay of the land and where bucks have been sighted in the past. Ranch hands and those who tend western crops are good sources if you can find them.

Quite often a western whitetail hunt may be a guided or outfitted hunt. In another chapter we discussed which questions you should ask concerning the area in which you plan to hunt. If you have done your homework and have selected a good outfitter or guide, listen to him concerning how he suggests that you hunt.

If you have enough faith in him to pay him good money in order to hunt with him on his property, have enough faith in him or her to hunt and do as they suggest. It's their home turf and if they are "worth their salt" and have your trust in booking with them, do as they suggest and in most every instance you're going to have a successful hunt.

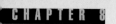

Long-Range Recon

The West's open spaces can be a challenge for many whitetail hunters because of the distance encountered in many shooting opportunities.

East

We had spent the morning hunting the thick hollow that runs off my farm and onto the Talladega National Forest. My son, Steve, and I were hunting a specific whitetail buck, a huge 12-point buck that we had come to call the Monarch of the Hollow.

It was several weeks after the peak of the rut and we were hunting thick hollows that the buck called home, using powerful short-range rifles. For this particular hunt, I was using a Thompson/Center Contender Carbine in a .375 Winchester caliber. This little rifle allowed me to slip through the thick brush easily and if a quick shot were necessary, this little rifle was up to it.

While the morning hunt was fun, it was unsuccessful as we only saw small bucks and does. Deciding to take a break and return to the cabin for lunch, we left the woods and entered a long narrow pasture. As I opened the pasture gate, I spotted the giant buck at the far end of the opening. He was looking at me. The doe he was with started running. Without thinking, I dropped down into a kneeling position shouldering the rifle. Finding the buck's shoulder in the scope, I took a breath, let part of it out, and squeezed the trigger. I could already see the big buck on my wall.

At the rifles report the buck, in no real hurry, trotted out of the pasture and into the brush, in the direction that the doe had disappeared.

"Your bullet hit the ground before it got to the buck," Steve said softly.

Looking at the distance to the end of the pasture where the big buck had been standing, I knew Steve was probably right. It turned out to be over 350 yards, not a shot for a 150-yard gun like the .375 Win.

A long-range shot was the last thing I expected on that cold December morning. In fact, there is only one place on my entire farm that you can get a 300-plus-yard shot and that was where I was standing when the Monarch showed himself.

THE EAST DOES HAVE LONG-RANGE SHOOTING

Contrary to the thinking of many hunters, there are many places in the eastern half of this country where 300- to 400-yard shots are possible for those equipped and trained to take them. Power line and gas line rights-of-ways are often good hunting areas, where trails cross the openings or where food plots are planted in the openings. Agricultural openings, such as my pasture and large fields, often offer long-range opportunities at big bucks. One of the longest one-shot kills I have ever made was in a large cutover cornfield. Forest clear-cuts, especially the second and third years after the cut, can present some challenging shooting. Older, mature woods are often open due to the high overhead canopy shading out the sunlight. In short, there are many opportunities for long-range shooting in the East.

BE PREPARED FOR LONG-RANGE SHOOTING

Any serious deer hunter should be prepared and have equipment for both short-range shooting and long-range shooting. Some people can make long-range gear do for short-range shooting, but the hunter equipped for hunting thick timber can't make his gear work very well for long-range shooting. In other words, the hunter using a .30-06 Springfield rifle with a 3-9X40 variable riflescope, 10X42 binoculars, and carrying X-sticks and rangefinder can, in a pinch, make a 75-yard shot. However, the hunter carrying a .30-30 Win. rifle with open sights and a 7X35 binocular will have a hard time evaluating and hitting a large buck at 300 yards.

Get to know the country you plan to hunt, and go equipped to shoot the range in which you are most likely to encounter a buck. Granted there will be the odd time, like the buck in my pasture, where you might get caught with the wrong gear, but most of the time you can plan for the anticipated shot. When you scout new whitetail territory, look at the terrain as you scout, and think about the shooting range for that country. Is it going to be mostly short-range hunting in heavy brush or is it mostly corn or soybean fields where the shots are likely going to be long? Plan accordingly. Match your gear to the terrain.

FIREARMS FOR LONG-RANGE SHOOTING

The wind blew large, heavy snowflakes into the dense Michigan cedar swamp where Don Miller was hunting. He cradled his Remington model 700 in .270 Win. caliber in his arms as he stalked through the thick brush. As he quietly picked his way between two snow-laden cedars, Miller saw a large eight-point buck standing in a small opening only 20 yards away. Miller started to mount the rifle, but the barrel caught in the thick cedar limbs. Seconds later and after much more motion, Miller got the rifle mounted, but couldn't find the buck in the riflescope which was turned up to 9-power. The buck saw the motion and bolted. Miller only got off one quick, missing shot from the rifle that he had sighted in for 200 yards.

In Virginia, Bert Danner had spent many weekends scouting a mountainous area. By opening day, he had patterned a buck that bedded in a huge laurel thicket at the head of a cove. The buck and several does used a trail that led from the laurels along a steep mountainside a quarter-mile away. Danner decided to take his .30-30 Win Model 94 and sit on an opposite slope where he would have a clear view of the deer trail. He didn't use a rangefinder and had no idea as to how far the trail was from his stand.

On opening morning, he spotted the buck slipping along the trail moving from the feeding area to the bedding area. His scouting was paying off. Danner shouldered the rifle and fired. The leaves some two feet below the buck seemed to explode where the bullet struck. It was a shot at over 300 yards. The buck disappeared over the mountaintop as Danner got off his second shot.

SELECT THE PROPER CALIBER RIFLE

The first rule of successful long-range shooting is to select a rifle and load in a caliber that is capable of taking enough energy to the 300-yard target to put the animal down in its tracks. If you hunt whitetail deer, mule deer, pronghorn, or other animals in their general size class, you will want a bullet with a downrange energy load of at least 1200 foot-pounds when it strikes the target. If you are hunting moose, caribou, elk, or black bear, your hunting bullet should strike the target with 2000 foot-pounds of energy. For grizzly hunting, 2800 foot-pounds of energy is advisable.

A good source to help you select a caliber suitable for long-range shooting is the ballistics tables found in ammunition catalogs published by such companies as Federal, Remington, and Winchester. These catalogs are usually available free from ammunitions dealers. The ballistics tables are easy to read and will quickly show you the long-range performance of a particular caliber with bullets of different weights. For example, by studying the Winchester catalog ballistics table, you will learn that the 7

Clear-cuts, such as the one shown above, are common in the East. For a few years, before replanted trees grow, these areas contain rich food sources for whitetails and offer excellent long-range hunting areas.

mm Rem. Mag., firing a Winchester Supreme load with a 139-grain soft point boat tail bullet, will deliver a 1944-foot-pound energy load at 300-yard zero; it has a trajectory of –6.3 inches at 300 yards and -18.3 inches at 400 yards. This information tells you this is an excellent long-range caliber.

HAVE A LIGHT, CREEP-FREE TRIGGER

Accurate long-range shooting is the result of shooter concentration and a steady rifle, and tantamount to both is a creep-free trigger with a lightweight pull. When you start to pull a trigger on a target some 300 yards out, the shooter's mind goes from good marksmanship concentration to wondering when the rifle will fire. The muscular effort that goes into pulling a difficult trigger creates motion, which transfers to rifle movement and misses.

Due to product liability problems, most hunting rifle manufacturers now ship their rifles with a trigger pull in the 7- to 10-pound range. This is too much for consistent long-range accuracy. Ideally, the long-range hunting rifle should have a trigger pull of 3 to 4 pounds. The trigger should also be free of creep, or travel between the point where you start pulling the trigger and where the trigger is when the

gun fires. Some of the better hunting rifles have adjustable triggers, which the shooter can adjust for pull and creep. If this is the case with your rifle, it is just a matter of reading the owner's manual and carefully making the adjustments. If your rifle does not have an adjustable trigger, you should have a qualified gunsmith install an adjustable trigger. It is a small price to pay for long-range accuracy.

I once guided an elk hunter who spent $5,000 on his elk hunt but refused to spend a few dollars on an adjustable trigger for his rifle. The trigger on his elk rifle had a 10-pound pull with lots of creep. Early one morning I put him within 250 yards of a bull in an open meadow. He missed the bull five times. I later discovered that his trigger was so bad he probably could not have hit the bull at 100 yards.

MATCH THE LOAD TO YOUR RIFLE

Whether you elect to use factory loads or hand loads, you must remember that each rifle has its own personality. The load that shoots well in your friend's pet .270 Win. may not shoot well in your .270, especially at long ranges. Take a variety of factory loads and/or hand loads to the range and determine which shoots most accurately in your rifle. Your goal should be to find a load that will keep a five-shot group inside 3 inches at 300 yards, and this will take some effort to find.

SIGHT-IN RIFLE FOR LONG-RANGE SHOOTING

One of the tricks to successful long-range shooting is sighting in your rifle so that when a target presents itself at 300 yards, you will not have to make any fast calculations to adjust your point of hold. Let's say you want to hunt whitetail deer with your Ruger 77 in .280 Rem. caliber, and the load it shoots best is a 150-grain Federal Premium factory load. Studying the ballistics chart in the Federal catalog tells you that with the load sighted in 1.8 inches high at 100 yards, the bullet will stay within an 8-inch circle out to 300 yards, well within the vital area of a big whitetail buck. This means you can shoot at a buck from 1 to 300 yards without having to think about adjusting your point of aim. Just place the center of the scope reticle on the shoulder and practice good marksmanship.

PRACTICE, PRACTICE, PRACTICE

Once you have the rifle sighted in for 300-yard shooting, the next step is to practice shooting at life-size animal targets on the species you plan to hunt. A good source of life-size big-game targets is the National Rifle Association.

Start out by practicing at 100 yards. Shoot at the target from the same position that you anticipate you will use on your hunt. For instance, if you plan to hunt whitetails from an elevated stand overlooking large agricultural fields, be sure to shoot from an elevated stand on your range. Concentrate on placing each bullet in the vitals. Simply hitting the deer target is not enough.

Next, go through the same exercise at 200 yards, and when that has been mastered, go out to 300 yards. It will be difficult at first to consistently place bullets in the vital area from a hunting position at 300 yards, but with practice and patience, it can be mastered.

DO NOT LEAVE RANGE ESTIMATION TO CHANCE

Most of the day was spent climbing a steep, treeless mountainside. At last, my guide and I were near the rockslide where a large Dall ram had rested during our climb.

We took off our hats and peered over the large rock that gave us cover from the ram's view. It was a magnificent sight, a full-curl ram within range of my .30-06. "Hold dead-on," my guide told me. "He's not over 150 yards away," the guide whispered. The big white sheep seemed farther away to me, but who was I to question a man who made his living at this game and on his terrain? Bedsides I was tired. In my excitement, I could already see the shoulder mount

over my fireplace.

I eased a round into the chamber of my rifle, which was sighted in 1 inch high at 100 yards, and prepared to ease back over the rock to take the shot I had worked so hard for. As I peered over the rock, the ram was walking slowly away, quartering up the rockslide to my left. My heart raced, and I centered the reticle of the riflescope on the ram's shoulder. "Hurry!" the guide hissed. "He's about to run."

The rifle cracked in the clear, thin mountain air, and I saw gravel explode close by the ram's feet. "He's further away than I thought," said the guide in disbelief. "Hold just over his back."

I worked the bolt once again and looked for the ram in the scope. He was running straight up the rockslide. I fired a second shot, then a third as the beautiful animal disappeared over the mountaintop, untouched.

The climb down the mountain that night was a sad ordeal for my

guide and me. After the shooting, we had paced off the distance to where the ram had been standing. The guide had missjudged the range considerably — it was 430 paces. Why hadn't I carried a rangefinder on that hunt?

Estimating distances, accurately, is a skill that is lacking in most hunters. The United States Army Artillery School found that no one is born with the ability to accurately judge distances, it must be learned. Since most of us don't have the opportunity to study the skill, we judge distances poorly.

Thanks to modern laser technology, there are now commercial rangefinders that can accurately give you distances out to 800 yards. These battery-operated rangefinders are small and lightweight making them easy to carry in a hunting coat or work jacket. In addition, they are affordable at prices ranging from $180 to about $400.

During this past fall I used the Bushnell Yardage Pro Compact

Simple crossed shooting sticks are easy to carry and can be set up quickly when shooting at long distances in open country.

Wayne Fears uses a handy pine tree and his hand as an improvised shooting rest to take aim in open country.

800 for getting accurate distances on my farm. At the press of a button it fires an eye-safe laser beam out to 800 yards to the selected subject and gives you, on an LED display, an instant reading, in yards or meters, as to distance to the subject. From measuring the size of fields to ponds to drainage ditch lengths, this simple to use rangefinder gave me accurate distances even though rain or foreground brush were often making it difficult to see. In each of the permanent hunting blinds on my farm, I used the rangefinder to read distances to permanent objects, such as a tree, a rock, or a stump, and recorded them inside the blind to help my guests make better-informed shooting decisions.

For hunting red deer on the treeless plains of Argentina this spring, our hunting party used compact Yardage Pro Scout rangefinders. Since most of the shots were long shots at 250- plus yards we were glad we had the small rangefinders. After this experience, a compact rangefinder will be in my hunting coat from now on when I am hunting whitetails in open country.

Companies that make rangefinders include Bushnell, Leica, Nikon, and Pentax. Most rangefinders have a 4- to 8-power viewfinder so that finding game in thick cover or at long distances is easy. In

addition, waterproof units will be available this year. Gone are the days when we must guess distances. Today's rangefinders take the guesswork out of it.

USE A RIFLE REST EVERY TIME

It is a proven fact that none of us can consistently shoot well at long ranges from an off-hand position. I have seen many big-game hunters shoot off-hand at animals standing broadside at ranges from 150 to 400 yards and never come close to their target.

To be a good long-distance shooter, it is going to take a good, solid rest for your rifle. Sometimes you will have a tree limb or a rock to use as a rest, but in open country where long-range shooting will most likely be necessary, rests are often scarce. You must take a rest with you. There are many available on the gun accessory market. Here are a few examples that are popular among long-distance shooters.

Harris Engineering Inc. makes the well-known Harris Bipods, two-legged metal supports that attach to the front sling swivel stud on the rifle. These legs are telescopic and fold out of the way under the barrel. When not needed, they may be quickly detached from the rifle.

Another company that makes a high-quality bipod

that attaches to the rifle swivel stud is the Caldwell Shooting Supplies bipod. They offer bipods that are designed for the prone position and the sitting position. I like these bipods because they allow the shooter to cant and swivel his rifle to make those last second adjustments.

Underwood Rifle and Pistol Rest Co. offers two sizes of folding cross sticks. These lightweight folding rests are quick to set up and fold down to a compact size, 13 inches, for easy carry. They come with a belt pouch for convenient carrying in the field. One size is for use from a sitting position, and the other is for shooting from a standing position.

I started using one of the Underwood sitting position cross sticks for handgun hunting and like it so well that I started using it for rifle hunting. I have taken a lot of whitetails at long distances thanks to these compact cross sticks.

Regardless of what type rest you choose for your hunting, plan on spending lots of time on the range shooting with it under your rifle. Learn to use it at distances out to 300-plus yards. If you plan on using a tree limb, rock, or fence post when hunting, then practice with the same on the range.

FOLLOW UP ALL SHOTS TAKEN

When shots are taken at long range, it is easy to think you have missed an animal. Hunters tend to think they have missed if the animal does not fall in its tracks, and recoil makes it especially easy not to be able to see the animal's reaction when you shoot at long ranges. Be sure to follow up every

shot as though you know you made a good hit. During my years of guiding, I saw many hunters fail to do a good job of checking around where the animal stood when they shot. We often found the buck several days later. If you are going to take long shots, then check out each shot before deciding it was a miss.

While I was working on this book I was hunting with friends on a cold, windy December morning when we came around the side of a mountain to see a buck easing under a rock ledge, some 250 yards away. He had no idea we were there. It was the final morning of the hunt and everyone had their buck except me. I got out my cross sticks and set up to make the shot. I asked one of my friends to spot for me as I shot. At the crack of the first shot I heard him say, "high, over his back."

I had taken off my gloves to take the difficult shot and now as I paused for the perfect second shot, my fingers were losing their feeling. I squeezed the trigger and the deer kept on walking. My friend said he didn't see where that shot went. As I prepared for a third shot the deer trotted over the side of the mountain and out of sight. "Both shots were clean misses," one of my friends stated. While it was probably so, I wanted to go study the area since I felt good about that second shot.

It was a long walk to get there, and it took us an hour or so trying to reconstruct the shot. I was about ready to admit to the misses when one of my friends announced he found a small spot of blood. To make a long story short, it took us some fancy trail-

ing but we found the buck dead down the side of the mountain. The second shot was a high lung shot and very fatal. However, if we had not taken the time to follow up the shot, this buck would have been wasted and I would have lost some of the confidence in my shooting. It pays to follow up every shot, especially long shots.

TALK YOURSELF THROUGH EACH SHOT

Anytime we see a large whitetail buck, or any other big-game animal, we get excited. That is natural. Without that excitement, the sport would not mean much to us. However, to shoot accurately at long ranges, we must control our excitement until after the shot.

The best way to do this is to talk yourself through each shot. Forget how the trophy will look over the fireplace; concentrate on the job at hand. Tell yourself to check the range. Next, make sure you have a solid rest for the rifle. Ask yourself if the path to the animal is free of limbs, grass, and other obstructions. Tell yourself to mount the rifle solidly and place the intersection of the reticle on the exact point of the animal you want to hit, or if it is a very long shot place the reticle intersection where you have been trained for that range. Allow for wind drift, if necessary. Take in a deep breath and let part of it out. Ease off the safety, and squeeeeeeeeeeeeeeze the trigger.

I still occasionally miss when taking a long-range shot. When I do, it is usually because in the excitement of the moment, I fail to talk myself through this little routine of good marksmanship.

West

"He's coming out from behind the small patch of sage brush about 350 yards away. Get ready," were my whispered instructions. The whitetail's habitat, consisting of dense woods and underbrush, was great fun to the hunter at my side. I intently watched the distant deer. He was an excellent western plains whitetail. The beams of his eight-point rack spread well beyond erect, forward hearing ears. His back tines were nearly twice the length of his ears and the next tines forward nearly as long. Brow tines were the same length as the measurement from his inner eyes to the tip of his nose.

He was a buck to write home about. I continued admiring him though my 10x Swarovski binoculars; still at the same time I wondered why I wasn't hearing a shot. Finally, I turned to look at my hunter. He stared alternately at the distant buck, his rifle, and me.

His rifle was a .300 Win Mag bolt action, topped with a high magnification variable scope. I didn't understand why he wasn't shooting. By then, the buck was standing broadside and offering the perfect shot. "What's the matter?" I finally quietly queried of my hunter. "Isn't he big enough?" I knew the buck would easily score in the mid-160s, even if he had only eight points. Talk about a huge buck!

"He's too far to shoot!" came his whispered reply. "I've never shot at a buck that far. I don't think I can hit him from here. Can we get closer?"

"He's only about 350 yards away and you've got a steady rest. I know your .300 Mag will kill a deer that far away because I've shot quite a few with that round at that distance and even farther." I hesitated, then again spoke, "I think you can take him." Then pointing out, "There's hardly enough cover to hide a rattlesnake between us and him. If we move, he's going to spook." I looked once again at the big eight-pointer. He was the kind of deer I loved and dreamed of taking. With my second look, I noticed how massive his antlers were. Even his tines were larger in circumference than were his eyes. His antlers at the base were nearly as big around as was his ear where it connected to his neck.

"I really think you should try to shoot the buck from here. I know you can do it! I'll tell you where to hold. Where will your bullet strike a target at 100 yards?"

My hunter responded, "Before I came out West I sighted it in to strike a target about 3 to $3^1/_2$ inches high at 100 yards. That's how Richard told me to sight-in. But I never shot it at anything beyond a hundred yards...."

"If that's the case put the cross hairs about a fourth of the way down from the top of his shoulder and gently pull the trigger. With that hold and the way your rifle is sighted you'll drop him in his tracks." I instructed, then continued, "Don't worry about wind drift because what little breeze there is, it's blowing directly from him to us."

I watched my hunter line up on the big whitetail using a boulder on which he laid his daypack where rested his rifle. Content he was settled down and on target, I returned my gaze toward the buck.

Although I was expecting the shot, it still surprised me when I heard the loud muzzle-braked rifle go off. Almost as quickly as the shot sounded I heard the reassuring and resounding "Plop!" of the bullet hitting the deer squarely on the shoulder. Moreover, just as quickly I saw the buck buckle and fall in his ample tracks. I knew immediately the bullet had broken the shoulder and undoubtedly done great damage to the deer's spinal column. When he went down, he didn't again move. He was essentially dead before he hit the ground.

I turned to look at my hunter. He was staring in total disbelief at his gun and then at the distant downed deer. As I congratulated him he kept saying, "I can't believe I shot a deer that far!"

I was truly tickled for him. My thoughts were "I can't believe you shot a deer that big." I knew this was a near record book buck and according to my hunter, his best buck ever before today was a spindly six-pointer that likely barely scored 90 B&C points. So not only had he made an excellent shot, he had taken a monstrous deer! As we walked toward the buck, he seemed to grow in size and antler dimensions. To be honest, when we finally got to his side, I was feeling a bit of jealousy! I dearly love massive beamed big eight-point bucks. This one was certainly that!

Hunting whitetail bucks in the wide open country look more like pronghorn antelope country than what many consider more typical. Throughout the white-tailed deer's western habitat there are many such areas that to the untrained and inexperienced eye look totally void of bucks, yet they hold big antlered and bodied whitetails.

Getting close to the prairie or open country a buck often takes a bit of "doing" and sometimes "fancy" shooting as well.

The first step in pursuing open country whitetails, especially in western habitats, is choosing and using a firearm that has long-range capabilities, not unlike eastern "bean field" rifles. Accuracy and downrange bullet performance are two key factors to consider.

Modern rifle calibers such as the various .300 Mags, 7mm Mags, as well as such cartridges as the .270 Winchester, .280 Remington, and the popular .30-06 Springfield are good choices. These calibers carry sufficient downrange energy out to 300 yards and beyond to cleanly bring down deer. We'll discuss calibers and caliber selection as well as downrange energy in another chapter. Suffice it to say here, these are good choices for western open country rifles.

For a rifle to be considered a long-range whitetail gun, it should be precisely accurate. That means you should be able to shoot less than 1-inch three-shot groups at 100 yards. Such accuracy will generally ensure at least 6- to 8-inch groups at 300 to 350 yards distant, and at least 8 to 9 or so inches at 400 yards. Over the years, I've shot some extremely accurate rifles that with a good solid rest and knowing the range, kept three shot at 500 yards within a 6-inch circle.

The vital area of most whitetails is about 10 inches in diameter. Rifles with lesser accuracy than described should not be considered long-range guns, and should not be shot at deer at longer ranges. Doing so simply increases the chances of wounding an animal, which is the last thing we as ethical hunters want to happen to the deer we love.

Rifles chambered for the various 7mm (.284) to .30 calibers (including the various magnums) are certainly capable of taking

In the West, distance judging can be difficult in vast, featureless country.

white-tailed deer at long ranges because of potential accuracy and downrange energy that causes severe tissue damage. However, it's the person who pulls the trigger that makes the shot. You can have the world's most accurate rifle, but if you do not shoot it well, it is just as well the world's most inaccurate rifle or handgun for that matter (since I dearly love hunting with handguns). Before heading out to hunt open country, whitetails spend considerable time at the range. Shoot a lot initially from a bench at measured ranges out to 400 yards and beyond to find out exactly where your bullet will strike a target at those distances. Learn your firearm's capabilities. Then start learning your own and your abilities with your firearms.

Once you've learned where and how accurately your rifle shoots, move away from the bench and learn how to take advantage of natural (in the field) rests or learn how to shoot from crossed shooting sticks such as those produced by Stoney Point. Until I started carrying Stoney Point's extendable Hunter Bipod, I spent half my time looking for a place to take a good solid rest and the rest of the time looking for game. With my Hunter Bipod, I've always got a solid rest handy regardless of whether I'm hunting in ankle-high grass or pockets of thin oak and sage that comes up to my waist.

With today's rangefinders, high-quality optics, shooting rests, and excellent bullets designed for long-range shooting, there is no reason not to take an occasional long shot, especially if

you cannot get any closer. Before even thinking of taking a long-range shot, know what you and your rifle are capable of doing.

Getting close to whitetails in wide-open country is as mentioned not always easy, especially in some terrain where vegetation is sparse, or, deer are feeding in huge hay fields. In the case of the latter, sometimes you can pattern deer and determine which trails they regularly take as they head to these fields late in the afternoon to feed on such crops as alfalfa. If that is the case, consider setting up a blind, possibly a ground blind near the field, perhaps a hundred of so yards downwind of the trail. However, the problem with that is bigger antlered and mature bucks do not necessarily stick to existing trails in such types of habitat. In relatively open country, mature bucks may approach a field one way today and from a totally different direction the next.

While hunting prairie whitetails with Richard Petrini on the rolling plains just a few miles east of Colorado Springs, Colorado, I heard of an extremely good eight-point buck that frequented a two-mile square (1280 acres) field planted in alfalfa. Problem was the buck, according to the ranch hand in charge of the property, never really approached the field from the same direction. However, he seemed to favor the northern portion of the field near where there were scattered hay bales.

The "situation" brought to mind a buck I had hunted in western Iowa the previous year during their late muzzleloader season. Every afternoon the buck appeared in a harvested cornfield,

where there was little cover. He approached the field by crossing a public road from the neighbor's property. The way he came into the field there was no way to ambush or approach him without being seen.

For a while I considered digging a pit and then covering myself with cornstalks. I would have done so, but the ground was frozen and digging a hole was out of the question. In addition, honestly, neither did I relish the thought of lying on icy ground for several hours.

I had three days left to hunt. Over a quick lunch with the farmer who owned the property, I lamented my dilemma. When up spoke the farmer, "Why don't you drag that grain hauling trailer over toward where the deer feeds each afternoon? They're used to seeing it."

He was right. The deer every afternoon walked within about 300 yards of the trailer. I had looked at it as a potential blind, but 300 yards was a bit farther than I wanted to shoot at a good deer with my .50 caliber muzzleloader.

Immediately after lunch, I drove to the deer field and moved the trailer to within about 200 yards of where the deer normally fed. That afternoon "my" buck returned as before but he stayed at least 250 yards from the trailer.

Next day I moved the trailer a bit closer to where the buck had been feeding, an area where there was a fair amount of corn left lying on the ground after the field had been harvested. The same thing happened that afternoon, except that the buck walked to within about 175 yards of where

I was hiding in the grain trailer. Unfortunately, when he did so, he was shielded by does and I did not risk taking a shot.

One afternoon remained before the season closed at sundown. At noon that last day, I moved the trailer about 50 yards closer to where he and a bunch of does had been regularly feeding. I could hear the proverbial robust lady warming up backstage.

It was a cold, gray afternoon. The thermometer hovered at the zero degree mark when I crawled into my grain trailer blind at two o'clock in the afternoon.

I had been there for about an hour and a half when the first does fed their way into the field from across the road. I noticed one was extremely big bodied. Through binoculars, I finally determined it was not a doe, but a buck that had apparently just shed his antlers, one of the potential downsides of hunting some of the late seasons in the Midwest. My first thoughts spoken in a whisper were "Oh no! My buck shed his antlers this morning." That's what exactly had happened to me the year before. By the time I finally determined how to get close enough for a muzzleloader shot at the buck I pursued, he had cast his antlers.

Then just when my deer emotions were at a serious low I spotted another buck crossing the road coming onto our property. A quick glance through the binoculars assured me it was the buck I had been hunting.

He slowly started feeding my way. Then it became a matter of wait and watch, alternately him and my wristwatch. The season ended at official sundown.

I felt confident with my .50 caliber muzzleloader out to about 150 or so yards. I would not shoot unless he came that close. Slowly he came. Check the watch. A few more steps in my direction; check the watch. Five more minutes before the season ended. But, the buck was still at about 175 yards. What to do? All I could do was wait and pray. Lo and behold the buck started walking my way.

Watch the buck, watch the clock. Watch the buck, watch the clock. On he came slowly closing to within the magic distance of 150 yards. The last few yards I watched anxiously through my scope with the cross hairs held firmly on the buck's quartering toward my shoulder. Then as if by magic or divine intervention, with about two minutes of legal shoot-

Larry Weishuhn uses one of the easily attached bipods that are available on the market. A bipod can serve as a great long-distance shooting aid when taking a shot in open country where natural rests are scarce or unavailable.

A laser or optical rangefinder is a great hunting aid for hunters in open country.

ing time remaining, the buck was 150 yards away and standing broadside. By then the wind had calmed a bit. With the muzzle-loader solidly rested on the edge of the grain trailer's sidewalls, I gently pulled the trigger, fire and smoke erupted from my muzzle. On the left side of the cloud of smoke I saw the buck run, take

about 20 steps, falter, and then fall. Finally the big ten-pointer was mine. My grain trailer buck remains one of my favorite all-time whitetail bucks, not only because he had a good rack but also because of what it took to take him and the genuine challenge he had presented me.

The memory of that hunt

prompted me to be innovative with trying to take the big eight-point eastern Colorado buck. I looked about the field; there was nothing to hide in front of, behind, or under. There was only one round hay bale on the entire field and it was at the other end of where the buck had been seen. What to do. I considered digging a pit to hide in,

the sides covered me but that I was still totally visible from above, where my orange could be seen. I laid straw around the sides to make it look like a big, though not tall, clump of grass.

I lay down in the field about two o'clock in the afternoon. Throughout the next couple of hours, I had pronghorn antelope feeding within about a hundred yards of me. As the evening progressed deer starting feeding on the edges and moving into the interior of the field where they apparently felt safe, both mule deer and whitetails.

About a half hour before sundown, the buck I desired walked into the field. He grazed for about 10 minutes within about a hundred yards. It was then I noticed he had broken one of his brows since he had last been seen. The broken tine didn't matter to me. I shot him from a rested prone position. Even though he was missing brow, the nearly 25-inch outside spread buck still gross scored in the low 160s on the B&C scoring system. I could not have been more pleased with the buck, nor with the way I had taken what had seemed at times an "untakable" prairie buck.

Hunting the West's hayfields is a good way to take a sizable open-country buck. One way to get closer to these bucks that feed among the hay bales is to create your own hay-bale blind, then moving it close to where the deer feed. Remember deer that feed in hayfields become used to feeding around bales of hay left in those fields.

To create your own hay-bale blind, start with a stiff single wire (about the diameter of a 16d nail) frame made of four hoops about 6 feet in diameter. Next, add six evenly spaced "staves" of straight pieces of the same stiff wire used to create the hoops. Tighten these to the hoops with softer "tie" wire available from your local hardware store. These staves should be about 7 feet long, which is about the same length as a hay bale. These staves give the "bale" frame some rigidity. Cover the frame with hardware cloth. Cut a door into the interior of the frame just large enough for you to comfortably get in and out of the blind. The last step is to weave grass stems through the many small holes to create a solid wall of natural grass all around the blind.

When you're finished, move the blind into the field you intend to hunt. Once you have it set up where you want it, set the bale up in an upright posi-

for several times in hunting eastern Wyoming I had hunted from a hand-dug pit where no other cover was available, with excellent success I might add. However, the ranch hand advised against it.

When I was about to run out of ideas he suggested laying down in the field and covering myself with a green tarp, but I wasn't sure that would be legal, since in doing so it would cover my required hunter's orange. Therefore, I decided to lay down in the field and make something of a nest out of the tarp, so that

tion, put a small chair into the blind, and then cut some openings in the hardware cloth which will allow you to see your surroundings and also poke your gun out for a shot. The great thing about these type of blinds is that they are relatively inexpensive to construct, and fairly easily moved. If deer start coming into the opposite of the field from where you are set up, you can easily move your blind into that area.

Once while hunting in northern Texas on the lower end of the Llano Estacado (Staked Plains), I used such a blind to perfection. Similar to the western Iowa buck, I learned about the buck from one of the ranch hands on the property. That knowledge and scouting set me back the cost of a bottle of adult libation. Doing so was an excellent investment.

Rangefinders, like this Leica LRF 900, use a laser beam to accurately measure ranges from 10 to 900 yards. Use of a rangefinder to determine distances to identifiable features around a tree stand or blind can be a valuable tactic in long-range shooting.

The buck frequented a big hay meadow in which there were still quite a few hay bales left in the field. I set up my hay-bale blind near where my scout had seen the buck several evenings in a row.

First afternoon of the hunt, the buck strode into the field. He mistook my blind for one of the hay bales that he had seen many times before. The shot was less than a hundred yards. The hay-bale blind worked to perfection.

The basics to remember when hunting open country whitetails are the same as hunting elsewhere, try to keep the wind in your face or quartering so, and whenever possible keep the sun at your back.

I dearly love hunting open country whitetails by spot and stalk. If you intend to do so, you need to resolve yourself to spending a lot of time simply sitting and glassing. Quite often big whitetails will hide in the smallest imaginable cover. I've seen even big-antlered buck hide where you would not have thought a jack rabbit could successfully hide from you.

When hunting open country, spend considerable amounts of time glassing. When hunting whitetails in this manner on the eastern plains or for that matter in the rolling hills of Canada or even Mexico, find a comfortable spot overlooking likely looking deer areas and even some not so likely looking deer areas and there, set up with your binoculars or spotting scope. Whether glassing for sheep or elk in the high country or whitetails on the rolling prairies, use a tripod in conjunction with your glassing. Not only will the tripod make a convenient rest for your binoculars, they will also help you set up a grid so you can truly glass an area.

I enjoy hunting both Carmen Mountain (fantails) and Coues whitetails in the rolling mountains of the Southwest. Hunting these diminutive subspecies of whitetails is much like hunting bighorn sheep. You spend hours and hours looking for them. And I can tell you if "regular" whitetails are good at hiding in a minimum of cover, these little deer will hide from you where there is virtually no cover.

Glassing for whitetails in open country is a lot like hunting deer in dense cover. Look for pieces of deer, the wiggle of a tail or ear, the sheen off of a moist nose, the glint of sunlight off of an antler, even the shadow of an antler or a part of the deer.

Use the glassing techniques whenever and wherever you hunt

open country whitetails.

One of the things about the open country is there is generally a fairly stiff breeze blowing; still days of little or no wind are generally quite rare. Wind can be both your ally and certainly your nemesis. If you are downwind of a deer there is naturally less chance he will smell you and less chance of him hearing you. Take advantage of the wind when and where you can!

Earlier we spoke about shooting long ranges at open country whitetails. Wind drift in terms of a bullet's flight is an interesting "deal." Normally I don't worry about it too much on the first shot unless the wind is quite strong and the distance quite long. If I'm concerned about potential problems the wind might cause, I will not shoot. Also, because I've hunted open country whitetails quite a bit, and I've made several mistakes in my formative whitetail years.

Quite a few years ago, I was hunting the diminutive Carmen Mountain subspecies mentioned earlier in the Chianti Mountains in Texas's Big Bend country. These are fairly open, though absolutely beautiful high desert-type mountains where often the little fantail whitetails cohabit with desert mule deer. They live in a beautiful, though often quite wind-blown habitat.

One afternoon, when the wind was blowing about 30 miles per hour with gusts up to 35 and 40, I spotted an extremely nice buck across a canyon. The buck straight across from one mountainside to the other was about 350 to 400 yards away. The open country in between the buck and me was not unlike a wind tunnel. I'm not sure what the velocity actually was. From a very rock-solid rest I took a shoot at the distant buck with a 130-grain fairly hot load .270 Winchester. I knew where the bullet should strike vertically at that distance and held accordingly. But then there was the gusty cross wind between my target and me that I was unsure of. Just for grins, I moved the cross hairs to an estimated three feet to the right and into the wind. I saw dust fly about 3 feet to the left of the deer. He looked in the direction the bullet struck and exploded a small rock. As he stared at it I bolted in another round and this time held about 6 feet into the wind. Again, I watched the bullet hit a rock about a foot to the left of the deer. It was close enough so that he moved, but only a few steps and again offered a broadside shot.

I bolted in a third round and this time allowed

Larry Weishuhn uses binoculars to search for whitetails in a deep river bottom in Texas' Chianti Mountains.

essentially for a wind drift of almost four of the little deer's body length into the wind. Shortly after the shot the little buck fell, but it was obvious by his movement he was hit a bit too far back. It took me a while to drop down the canyon wall and scale the other side to get to within reasonable shooting distance of the deer to finish him off. I felt horrible about what I had done and swore never again to take a shot where I was unsure how much the bullet would drift with the wind.

These days when taking a long shot I hardly ever shoot at a deer or any other animal if the breeze isn't blowing either from the animal toward me, or in some instances when the breeze is blowing from me to it. I also, do not take ashot through a cross wind at beyond about 250 yards if the wind exceeds much over about 10 miles per hour. If it's blowing harder I'll try to get closer.

Hunting open country whitetails is exciting, challenging, and ever changing. Hunting this type of terrain and habitat, like others, requires being adaptable. As conditions change, so should hunting techniques.

Penetrating the Thick Stuff

Introduced deer browse, such as this well-fertilized tangle of honeysuckle growing near an area of thick cover, can draw deer like a magnet.

East

Mention eastern whitetail hunting to a westerner and he will probably think of swamps and head-high fields of corn. While there is plenty of open country deer hunting in the East, there are those places that require a different way of thinking and short-range firearms.

Deer hunting thick growth, like hunting any other area, simply requires the hunter to find out what the deer are doing and then set up to get a shot. Locating the food source is one quick way to solve the thick cover problem.

Many years ago, while working as a wildlife manager in south Georgia, I was helping run the first bowhunt on an 80,000-acre wildlife management area. The area was near the Okefenokee Swamp and was forested with pine and oak trees. The understory was a jungle of gallberry and palmetto. For the first few days of the hunt, not one buck was checked in. The hunters couldn't figure out what the deer were feeding on. Most were hunting around the scattered oaks but there were very few acorns that year.

One night around a campfire in the hunter's campground, well-known bowhunter Dan Quillian asked me what type of soft mast might be available to the deer in the management area. After giving it some

thought, I remembered that the palmetto plants found along a low ridge in the area had an abundant crop of berries, and I knew that deer were fond of those fruity berries. The next day, Quillian and some of the other bowhunters started scouting the ridge. When they found the palmettos bearing fruit, they found deer. Suddenly we had deer at the checking station.

CLEAR-CUTS

Perhaps one of the thickest deer areas to hunt in the East is in a clear-cut block that is in the years 5 through 12 of regrowth. In much of the East it will be growing back in planted pine. During this growth period the clear-cut block becomes a favorite bedding area and safety area for deer and is almost impossible for a hunter to walk through it, much less hunt in it.

At this stage of growth in a clear-cut, any openings out in the block can be a deer hunting hot spot. Areas such as hardwood islands, pockets of wetland, creeks, open areas where the replanted trees have died. or areas that the planters missed offer excellent locations for a blind. I once found a one-acre opening out in a block of eight-year-old pines in South Carolina. The area was grown up in sweet gum saplings and honeysuckle. That summer I went into the area, cut the saplings down, and fertilized the honeysuckle. Just before the deer season opened, I went into the area and set up a ground blind.

The first day I sat in the blind I watched deer come to the opening all day long. It was an oasis of quality food in the middle of acres of pine cover, which offered little of food value.

The second morning long before daylight, I made my way to the blind and set up for a day of hunting. No sooner had the first rays of daylight begun to show in the east, it began to pour rain. I broke out my rain suit and made the decision to hunt all day rain or no rain. By noon, I questioned my decision as I was wet and had not seen so much as a doe. As I sat thinking about my warm, dry truck a few hundred yards away, a nine-point buck eased out into the clearing and started feeding. I couldn't get my T/C Contender handgun up fast enough. My island in a sea of pines paid off. Two more nice bucks were taken from that stand that season.

A really good hunter whom I have hunted with in clear-cuts is Ted Salters of Bessemer, Alabama. Ted goes into the center of a thick clear-cut and scouts for a point where several heavily used deer trails cross. Here he will cut an open lane some 10 feet wide and 20 to 30 yards long. This lane is a shooting lane. Next Ted builds a ground blind looking down the lane. He spends the day in the blind with his rifle in a ready position. He has found that the bucks travel in the thick cover all day, feeling secure. When they

Hunting in the lanes of cornfields can be productive for the patient hunter.

come to the opening they step into it and pause for a few moments to look down the opening. It works as Ted has taken some really good bucks using this technique. His young daughter took her first buck from one of Ted's blinds. A buck most deer hunters would dream about.

I have a friend in Illinois who uses a technique similar to Ted's in the vast cornfields on his farm. He cuts lanes through some of his larger cornfields early in the fall to move farm equipment through the fields. He has found that by watching these lanes he catches bucks stopping to look when

crossing the opening. He likes this method of stand hunting better than the man drives and still hunting he used to use to try to get the big corn-fed bucks.

CREEK BOTTOMS
The East has many buck rich habitats that are never hunted and that are the thick creek bottoms found in all areas. Some are narrow and others are quite wide. Usually they are hunted a lot around the edge but few hunters go into the thickets due to the limited visibility and the tangle of vegetation that must be negotiated. Because of this, the creek jungles become buck bedrooms.

The East has many prime buck habitats that are rarely hunted, such as this tangled creek bottom in the pine woods of the Southeast.

A hunter fires from his portable stand in a southern pine plantation. Using a tree stand to look down into thick cover can be a productive way to find big buck.

I have two friends in Louisiana who specialize in hunting thick creek bottoms. They have developed a two-man drive, which works well under certain conditions and has produced some nice bucks. They select a creek bottom that has a logging road or field edge running parallel to the edge of the bottom. One of the hunters will ease along the open edge at a very slow pace. The second hunter walks parallel to the edge as quietly as possible through the thick cover at a distance from 50 to 100 yards from the edge. These hunters try to stay abreast of one another. When the hunter in the thick cover gets a deer up, it usually is not spooked too badly and gets up well in front of him. Often the hunter will never see the deer.

Many times the deer will trot out into the open edge and stop to see what was moving in the cover. The outside hunter takes his shot.

As with all drives, this type drive requires extremely safe hunting practices, and hunter orange must be worn.

Another hunter I know that hunts the thickest of creek bottoms successfully is Ken Gates of Aliceville, Alabama. Each year he takes several heavy-racked bucks by taking a portable tree stand into the thickest creek bottom he can find. He climbs a tree where he can see into the thick area and allows other hunters to do their moving in the areas around the edge. It requires several days per buck, but his patience pays off. As he sits there overlooking the

thick cover, he sees big bucks responding to the heavy hunting pressure secretly moving about their creek bottom hideouts.

After Ken told me about his creek bottom method of hunting, I decided to give it a try. I had a creek bottom on my property that was just about as thick as it can get. Much of the bottom was grown up in cane. I knew there was a lot of deer staying in the bottom so I took a portable tree stand and climbed up a tall water oak high enough to see down into the cane. Once I got into position, I realized I stood out on the side of the tree like a sore thumb, but decided to put on my camo head net and gloves and try it anyway.

Just before dark, I could see the cane parting as something moved toward me. I got my bow ready, knocked an arrow, and watched with heart pounding as the cane parted closer and closer. As the cane parted in front of me, I looked down to see a buck crawling through on his knees with his head laid back. I took a shot, but my arrow went over his back. The buck broke into a run and got away. He had spotted me and tried to get by me without being seen. I would never have known he was there if I hadn't seen the cane parting.

One year I was hunting on a hunting club lease that had a thick creek bottom on the property. Members of the club knew there were bucks using the jungle and several club members had attempted to hunt in there but it was just too thick. One day it was too windy to hunt so I borrowed a canoe from a nearby farmer and floated the creek. I say floated but it was more like drag than float as the creek was very shallow in places and had high steep banks. For almost a mile, the banks of the creek were so steep that it would have been almost impossible for deer to cross. Then I came to a sudden dip in both banks. There was a deer trail that looked like a cattle cross-

ing. I took a GPS reading, marked the crossing on a map, and finished my canoe trip. The next day I spent opening and marking a trail to the crossing so I could get to it in the dark. On Christmas Eve morning, I was sitting on the creek bank some 30 yards above the crossing with a Marlin .45-70 open sighted rifle in my hands. The wind was right and I was dressed in camo. That morning I saw 16 does and three bucks cross the creek within the first three hours of daylight. One of those bucks was a tall, heavy-racked eight-point buck that stopped on the bank of the creek just before entering the water. I took the clear shot. I spent the rest of the day getting the buck out to where I could get my four-wheeler.

Hunting in thick eastern deer habitat requires a lot of thought and planning since you will often be in close proximity to deer. Watching the wind is most critical in this type of cover. Camo clothing becomes more important and having a portable tree stand can be an important tool. I like to wear yellow shooting glasses when hunting these areas to help brighten up the cover I will be scanning when low light conditions occur.

Thick cover requires the use of camouflage and a short-range rifle or shotgun.

West

"Ouch!" came the pained low voice from behind me, followed by a groan, moan, and then, "No way a big buck could get through this mess. It's simply too thick with too many thorns. No self-respecting whitetail buck would ever hide in this thicket, no way!"

"Shhhhhh!" I cautioned in a whisper, "Jim we're only about a hundred yards away from where I want to set up and rattle. It's a small opening in the middle of this gahawful myriad of thorns and spines. Conditions including the wind are right and if you'll follow me quietly the rest of the way, I think you'll be happy you did."

Jim Spence had come to the famed Brush Country in search of a big whitetail buck. After years of hunting in his native Pennsylvania and in some of the adjoining states, he had come to Texas, lured there by tales he had read in such publications as *North American Whitetail* and others. He had often hunted thickets back home but seldom thickets as dense as what we literally snaked our way through at the moment. And I doubted seriously he had ever encountered more sharp spines and thorns.

Ten minutes later we had sneaked into a small brush studded opening roughly the size of half a football field, or about 40 yards by 50 yards. We eased into the center of the grassy opening scattered with mesquite trees and sat down, and I instructed Jim to watch downwind. I waited for about 20 minutes before starting to "work" the horns, setting up a scenario of two aggressive, mature bucks meeting.

After a bit of rubbing of antlers on a nearby mesquite, doing some soft grunting, and then making a snort-wheeze, I slammed the antlers together while at the same time pushing and shoving with my boot heels into anything close by.

Immediately a good ten-pointer charged out of the brush. Jim looked back at me and I wagged my head in a negative manner, yet never stopped meshing the horns together. As the buck stood about 20 steps away watching, I continued rattling, and then started many a loud grunting noises with my mouth to sound like an old mature buck really getting into the fight. My loud grunt was not yet finished when I saw movement coming our way, approaching directly downwind of our position. Jim saw the deer at the same time. Immediately upon completing my loud groan I whispered, "Shoot!" Jim obeyed my instruction. The shot was true and the deer fell before it made it back to the edge of the thick brush. When he looked back at me the expression in his eyes and on his face said it all! Moments later we approached a true "muy grande de brasada," the kind of bucks the South Texas Brush Country had become famous for producing.

Closer inspection revealed the buck had a total of 18 points. He was a basic 6 by 5 with 7 nontypical points, including split tines and two- to three-inch long points between the brow tines and the burr. His rack was a deep mahogany color with ivory colored polished tips. His mass like his tine length were impressive. Bases were nearly 6 inches in circumference and his beams carried great mass all the way to the tips. Tines were long, the longest being nearly 13 inches. His outside spread was easily 24 inches. Here was a buck to write home about, to regale around campfires wherever whitetail hunters gathered. "Was the crawl through the thorns and getting your hide pierced a few times worth it?" I asked Jim. With a wide smile he simply replied, "What thorns?"

Hunting thick cover can truly be worth the effort of getting there. But if you have noticed, I described hunting inside thick cover and not necessarily in it. Had we tried to rattle in the thickest of the cover, chances are if we had attracted the old buck, we would never have seen him before he would have caught our scent.

I dearly love hunting and especially rattling near thick cover, but not necessarily in cover so thick I can't see anything when it approaches. In almost every thicket, somewhere within it is an opening that affords some visibility and it's these areas I look for when hunting thickets.

THE MAGIC OF SENDEROS

Over the years of hunting thick cover from the Brush Country of South Texas and northern Mexico to the dark timber and Provincial Forest of western Canada, I have learned that although the vegetation is extremely different, the techniques to hunt such thick cover are relatively similar.

In the arid brush-infested areas of the Southwest the only visual access to some of the thickets, although the vegetation may only be 8 to 12 feet tall, are roads or pathways cut through the brush. Quite often these *senderos* were cut by dozer drivers employed by petroleum companies in preparation for doing seismic work in the area. Other times these *senderos* may be opened for fence lines or access to other parts of the property. In the tree-covered areas of the Northwest sometimes again the only openings are roads cut through the tall trees for the same purposes. Deer in both places tend to cross such paths or *senderos* and quite often use them as trails or travel ways.

My favored way of hunting *senderos* whether in the Northwest or Southwest is from highly mobile tripods. These can be quickly moved into an area and if necessary can be moved up or down the *sendero* depending upon where the great deer activity occurs.

Tripods also work well in other areas of the West where sometimes the best place to hunt is above the ground so you can cover more territory. Simply set the tripod up against some existing structure such as a mesquite or tall shrub that would never support any kind of tree stand and you've got a great hunting blind. The added height, say 8 to 10 feet off of the ground serves as a great observation platform.

ESTABLISH YOUR OWN DEER TRAIL

Deer, like people, when in thick cover tend to follow the path of least resistance. Remember also if you hunt thick cover, you have to be able to see a deer in order to shoot him. So why not establish your own trail through thickets and thick cover and lead the deer where you want them to go, such as in by your stand.

The best time to establish a trail through a thicket is during late winter through early summer. Do so by simply hacking a trail through the thicket, making it about 6 feet or so wide. Lay the trail out taking into consideration what the prevailing wind will be during the fall when you're hunting. And rather than a straight path let the trail "snake" a bit so that it goes by where you plan to set up later in the fall. While laying out the trail, pick a couple of stand locations taking into consideration wind directions so you can hunt the area regardless of which way the wind is blowing.

Once you've established the trail and cut the vegetation down to ground level, it will likely put out highly nutritious and palatable shoots. If legal in your area these can be "sweetened" a bit by applying a broad base commercial fertilizer such as 13-13-13 available at the local feed and seed or nursery store.

Establishing such trails through thick cover has led to the taking of several big bucks on the properties I've managed and hunted.

HUNTING THICK BEDDING COVER

One of the toughest bucks I ever hunted was an old mature six-pointer that was a prolific breeder and tended to pass his six-point rack genes on to his offspring. He lived on a ranch in Texas that we intensively managed for quality deer. I hunted hard for this particular deer in hopes of removing him from the herd. I tried everything that was legal, including baiting. Nothing worked. To make matters worse, the only time I saw the deer was at night when I was doing research or when he happened to run across the

Larry Weishuhn's favorite way to hunt *senderos*, narrow lanes cut through the Brush Country of South Texas and Mexico, is by using a 10-foot tripod.

pasture road in front of one of our vehicles. I was nearly at wit's end.

Finally, while on a scouting mission near where I suspected he lived, I walked into a dense, 30 yards square, oak brush thicket. There I found two of the buck's shed antlers from years past and several recent and well-used beds. I decided the best way to hunt the deer was to get right into his bedroom in the thicket. I would be able to do so only under the right conditions, which meant getting into the thicket well before first light and being able to do so undetected and remaining so as I waited for him.

Two days later a blustery cold front blew in at about midnight. I got up just before three that morning, dressed warmly and headed to the thicket and sat down on the leeward side of the center.

About an hour before first light I heard a deer walk into the thicket and bed down only about 10 or 12 feet upwind of where I was sitting with my back against a small oak sapling and facing into the wind. The wait until first and legal shooting light was a

long one. As black turned to gray I could see the deer. It was the buck I was after and he was laying down facing into the wind and away from me.

Each time there was a particularly blustery blast of frigid north wind I eased my rifle a bit more into shooting position and finally I could see the deer and the sights of my open-sighted .30-30, chosen because it was short and I knew my shot, if indeed it came, would be close. When another cold blast blew through the thicket, I thumbed back the hammer. I noticed the buck cup his ear back toward the metallic sound but by then it was too late. Finally I had taken him. He was not big of antler but he remains one of my more challenging trophies ever collected.

Would the same technique work again elsewhere? I can assure you I learned an excellent lesson with that buck and it has helped me take numerous other dense cover bucks.

A FOREST OF CORNSTALKS

Ever hunted standing corn before it was harvested? Talk about a thicket and dense cover! If you thought some of the swamps in Alabama were close in cover, or the Brush Country of South Texas was difficult to hunt because of the brush, consider hunting standing corn.

I learned about hunting standing corn on a hunt to eastern Wyoming. The outfitter, Rich Edwards, had gained access to a chunk of prairie country traversed by several tulle-choked creeks which bordered several cornfields. According to Rich the area held some truly impressive corn-fed bucks. But he warned hunting them was going to be in thick and tight quarters.

Growing up where I did in Texas we had a few cornfields in our area but thanks to a rather long growing season, by the time hunting season came along, all the corn had been harvested and had either been plowed under or grazed upon by cattle to the point they were no longer of any interest to deer.

"Hunting standing corn is easy," Rich told me the night before I was to hunt the cornfields. "You simply start downwind and slowly walk into the wind. Ease forward and peer left and right each time you step into a new row. Deer bed between rows quite frequently and sometimes you can catch one napping or looking the other way. There's usually not too much time to evaluate and shoot when you do see a deer. But you know what a good buck looks like. If you see one that you want, shoot him!"

It all sounded simple enough. It was not quite that simple, and it certainly added a new dimension to hunting deer in thick cover. That first day I spooked several deer, including one truly nice buck. Toward the end of the day I realized my biggest problem was that I had been moving too quickly through the rows.

The next day I hunted the other end of the same property. Near the center of about a 20-acre field I spotted a sizable buck lying down between rows. I shot him at less than 15 yards. Interesting hunt!

GRASSLAND THICKETS

Throughout much of the West, farmers are restoring portions of their croplands into grasslands such as they were a couple of centuries ago. This has been done through the government's CRP program, which pays landowners not to farm their country and helps them reestablish the tall grass prairie it once was.

Most hunters might consider a prairie thick cover, unless they have hunted some of the taller grass CRP lands. Some grasses like Indian grass, big bluestem, and others can grow to six feet or taller.

CRP land often borders highly productive farmland and while deer don't eat tall grass they certainly use these tall grass pastures as bedding areas. Hunting deer in these situations can be both a blessing and a curse.

Thankfully some of the CRP lands have vantage points where you can set up to glass, looking for antler tips, sticking up out of the grass. Once you've located antler tips the stalk is on.

Plan your stalk with the wind in your face and the sun, if shining, at your back. Move slowly and deliberately. The biggest problem is, once you've located the buck you want to pursue from a distance, finding him when you get close.

I've hunted CRP lands in eastern Colorado and Kansas. The bucks in these areas tend to be big, both in terms of body and antler. I'm still looking to take my first CRP buck. When I finally do take one, I know he'll be a "thick cover" buck whose mounted antlers I will definitely want to put on my wall.

Large fields of standing corn can present some of the thickest deer habitat that a hunter will encounter.

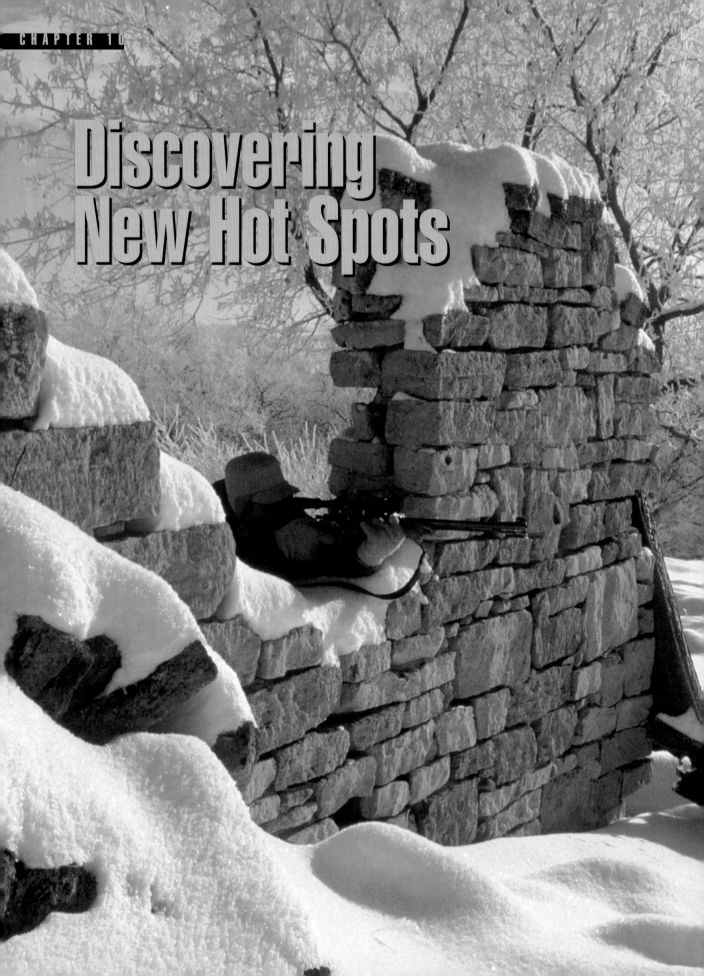

Discovering New Hot Spots

A ruined house makes an excellent improvised deer blind. Overlooked bucks can be found in unexpected places such as near highways and ranch gates.

East

During a past hunting season when I lived in Georgia, a friend and I were planning a hunt for whitetails in a national forest. I was to pick him up at his home on the edge of a city of 55,000 people, and then we would continue the trip another 75 miles to the forest for the daylong hunt. At 2 a.m. as I approached his house, my headlights picked up a nice eight-point buck standing on an embankment overlooking the highway.

When I reached my friend's house, the first thing I said to him was, "Why are we driving half the night to hunt when you've got good bucks right here at your house?" He looked amazed and thought I was kidding. He was shocked to hear what I had seen. Near his house, where I had seen the buck, was a tract of land that had been clear-cut and set out in pine trees. Due to that activity, plus the fact that there were a number of houses in the vicinity, he had never scouted the area even though he had a permit to bowhunt there. We went on with our planned hunt and didn't take a buck, but during the next three weeks, my friend took two, almost within sight of his house.

All too often, we overlook outstanding hunting right under our noses. Here in the East, whitetail deer have adapted to living close to man, even in subdivisions, without man ever realizing it. I live in a town of 4,000 and a nice ten-point buck was taken, illegally, in the middle of our town last year. I have seen some nice bucks while looking out the windows of the North American Hunting Club building while there on business. These offices are in a busy suburb of Minneapolis.

When I owned Stagshead Lodge in Alabama, I was amazed at the number of nice bucks that spent most of the hunting season around the lodge facilities. Several deer stayed in the impact area of the rifle range. One of the nicest bucks I saw on the property spent an entire hunting season near our butcher building. Since none of my hunting clients wanted to hunt near the lodge compound, always in remote areas, the deer around the lodge were safe.

At another hunting lodge, which I managed for several years, some of the best hunting was in a narrow strip of woods between a major U.S. highway and a large clear-cut area. None of the hunters felt that this would be a good place to hunt, and rarely did anyone go into these woods. However, when our biologists checked the woods out, they found that several extremely large bucks were holding up in this little patch of woods during the day, making it a great place to take a stand.

Within a public hunting area that I managed several years ago, I saw a similar situation. The best bucks that we saw each year always spent the hunting seasons around the checking station because no one ever hunted there.

OVERLOOKED BUCKS REACT TO MAN

Deer, unlike people, don't reason; their behavior is simply reaction to what's going on around them. They quickly become conditioned to move when the human activities are at a minimum, such as midday or at night. They can spend their entire lives near subdivisions, farms, and other places inhabited by man and rarely be seen.

Their survival instinct causes them to not only pattern their movements to times when it is safe, but to retreat to undisturbed areas that are overlooked by many hunters. These areas may include a grown-up fencerow, a thick wood lot, a cornfield with standing stalks, overgrown ditches and gulleys, beaver swamps, stream or creek banks grown thick with cane or vines, planted pines, and overgrown areas around old buildings or abandoned farm equipment. Deer, especially older bucks, are quick to retreat to the relative safety of such areas and only move out of them to feed or to seek does during the rut.

USE YOUR SCOUTING SKILLS

Since these wary overlooked bucks don't expose themselves too often, some scouting skills are required to find their general location and get a pattern on their movements. One

Well-developed scouting skills are required to pattern overlooked bucks.

of the first signs to look for are deer tracks. While they can't tell you the sex of the animal, tracks can let you know that deer are moving about in an area that you may not have suspected deer being in.

One of the best bucks I ever took with a bow was taken at a small farm near where I was going to college. The farmer who owned the farm let me shoot rabbits with a shotgun on the backside away from where he kept his cattle. One afternoon as I opened a gate at his barn, I happened to see deer tracks mixed in with cattle tracks. When I asked him about them, he told me he occasionally saw deer around his barn, but not many. He gave me permission to bow-hunt, and on my second afternoon I took a nice seven-pointer from a stand in the hayloft. Two other bucks were out in the barn lot at the time I shot. The deer were moving out of a thick wood lot to a small patch of grass planted next to the barn.

Once it is determined that deer are present, the next sign to scout for is trails leading from bedding to feeding areas. Overlooked deer are wary all the time and are masters of concealment even when moving. Look for their trails to

wind along thick fencerows, through planted pines or thick wood lots, or along the edges of grown-up fields. These deer don't feel comfortable out in the open.

The trails may be heavily used if the food source is available for long periods. In upstate New York, I have seen some secluded deer trails used so much that they looked like cattle trails. These led to a constant source of choice food, such as a winter pasture. In one case, I found a farmer feeding corn to his hogs.

When scouting for trails be on the constant alert for possible feeding areas. Learn what native foods in your area the deer like. Be able to identify that food source in the field. Where I live, the persimmon tree bearing fruit during bow season will draw deer like flies to an outhouse, but if you can't identify persimmon, you may overlook an excellent stand site.

If you find a likely food source, say a grove of white oak trees with a good mast crop or an alfalfa field, look for tracks. Also, look for droppings. A lot of deer droppings that have been there for various lengths of time indicate that deer are feeding there often.

Once the food source is found, try to find the trail used by the deer to reach the food. As is in the case of an agricultural crop, it may not be apparent at the edge of the field, but farther back into the woods a heavily used trail may be found. Take your time and do a good job of scouting.

TIMING IS EVERYTHING

When you find a deer trail, you may want to determine if it's being used. Try tying a dark piece of sewing thread across the trail at waist height. Check the thread daily to see if deer moving along the trail break the thread. If so, locate a site for a portable tree stand or ground blind. A trail camera would be good to use in this situation.

The type of pressure from man will play a major role in when overlooked bucks will move. If it is pressure from other hunters, then the deer may move at midday if that's when most of the hunters leave the woods to go to work or to return to their vehicles for lunch and naps. If there is pressure from a construction crew or logging crew, the period of movement may be after quitting time. Study the quietest time of the day and hunt then.

If the deer seem to be moving mostly at night, concentrate your hunting at daybreak when they will be returning from feeding and at dusk when they will begin moving to feed.

A good area to look for when hunting wary overlooked eastern bucks is an extremely thick area around water, such as edges along riverbanks or grown-up creek bottoms. Deer feel safe in such areas and will often move around in them during the day. Those who hunt from portable tree stands would be wise to seek out thickets of this type where there is deer sign, put up their tree stands where they can look

Wayne Fears and Fred Bear used a canoe to get into this remote swamp while bowhunting for whitetails.

down into the thickets, and spend the entire day watching. Granted, they may see fewer deer than hunters who have vast open areas to watch, but when they do see a deer, it may well be a buck within bow range.

BIG BUCKS NEVER HAVE DRY FEET

One of the best spots for locating deer in populated areas is in swamps created by the dam-building activity of beavers. The water, which doesn't bother the deer, keeps people out. Bucks will take refuge in the swamp using dry islands and mounds around trees to bed on. Most swamps have an abundance of deer food, which lets the bucks hide in comfort.

I like to wade or take a canoe into these areas that most hunters will not bother to enter due to the thickness of the vegetation, remoteness, or dislike of the wet environment. Almost any island or dry patch of ground can be a good location for a stand.

Dry areas in swamps will often be covered with deer sign. It is not unusual to find trails leading out of the water, pressed-down leaves where bedding has occurred, and droppings that have been there for various periods of time. This indicates frequent use.

When possible, I like to use my camouflage canoe in these areas. It makes carrying a portable tree stand easy, and deer pay very little attention to the quiet, slow-moving canoe. In addition, when you take a large buck it makes getting him out much easier.

When hunting in the surrounding area is heavy, it is not unusual for several bucks to move into a

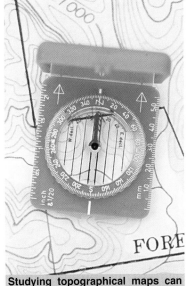
Studying topographical maps can help you locate overlooked bucks.

beaver swamp. This, in effect, has the other hunters working for you.

MAP YOUR WAY TO SUCCESS

A U.S.G.S. topo map can be a great aid in helping you find likely locations for overlooked deer movement. I was recently on a hunt in an area that was made up of small apple farms. The deer in the area were spooky, having been run off by the landowners many times. I was at a loss as to where to start hunting, so I turned to a topo map and began to study it carefully. Suddenly, it jumped out at me that there was a narrow band of woods between a large orchard and an interstate highway. It appeared to me that few people would have reason to go into those woods. I went there and found a well-used deer trail. I placed my portable tree stand in the center of this corridor, and on the first day of hunting, I took a fat six-pointer.

USE PORTABLE TREE STANDS

By now, it is obvious that I like to use a portable tree stand for hunting overlooked bucks. As we stat-

ed in the beginning, these animals can be extremely wary, perhaps not from being hunted, but from living in close proximity to man. Their senses are what keep them alive. The hunter on an elevated tree stand has the advantage of keeping his scent above the animal. Being cautious of the wind direction when putting up the tree stand and wearing a cover scent assures you of seeing more deer. Another benefit of the portable tree stand is concealment. Many deer will pass near the tree stand and never look at the human mass that is perched up in the tree above their eye level. Of course, occasionally a deer might look up and spot the hunter, especially if the hunter does not have the ability to remain motionless. However, the conscientious hunter who places his tree stand some 12 to 20 feet above the ground definitely has an advantage over many of the deer that will be walking by.

Height also gives us the ability to look down into areas. In extremely thick prime hunting areas, such as cane bottoms along creeks, thick beaver swamps with lots of underbrush, blowdowns, thick palmetto ground cover, and areas that otherwise would be almost impossible to hunt from the ground, the hunter using a portable tree stand can select a well-positioned tree, go up, and look down into the thick areas in which bucks like to travel.

While this chapter addresses mostly early season ambush tactics, the overlooked buck hunter should be aware that when the rut occurs, the overlooked buck will become less wary. He will throw caution to the wind and

Portable tree stands are a valuable tool to use in hunting overlooked bucks.

may be seen at any time of the day. Learn to locate active scrapes and go prepared to watch these scrapes all day for as many as three consecutive days. There is no question that the best time to hunt these bucks is during the rut.

There are some real advantages to being an overlooked buck hunter. Some of the best hunts I've ever been on were for deer in populated areas. Hunting was permitted "for bow only" for safety reasons. I once had the opportunity to hunt a college campus during Christmas break. The overpopulated deer were eating everything green on campus. I have hunted next to subdivisions and in military ammo storage areas. All were choice hunts.

A friend of mine has a 1,000-acre bow hunting-only lease inside the city limits of a city of 100,000 people. The bank which manages the land uses the bowhunters to keep the deer population within the carrying capacity of the land. My friend tells me that the deer on this property, surrounded on three sides by expensive homes, know a lot about people and it takes some unusual tactics to get a shot.

Regardless of where you find wary and overlooked bucks, good scouting, proper location of a portable tree stand, and hunting when the deer feel safe to move can give you a lot of hunting fun and put venison on the table.

Here in the East where subdivisions are springing up everywhere and deer are becoming more of a problem for homeowners, you can bet there are going to be some unusual opportunities for hunters to hunt these urban deer.

West

The term "overlooked whitetails" covers a w-i-d-e territory. Quite often these overlooked bucks are wellantlered because they've had the opportunity to mature and grow big. Sometimes they exist in the darnedest places, such as practically under our noses or in areas that most well-educated deer hunters avoid because they know no self-respecting buck would live in such places. Right.

Regardless of where you hunt, how many times have you seen big whitetail bucks standing beside heavy-traffic highways, or near or within the city limits of a major metropolis, or crossing the road when you stop to open the gate leading to the property you plan on hunting? Or for that matter how many times have you driven past a big grassy field headed to your favorite deer stand? You know no buck would bed in such a field because simply there is too little cover. Or, how about when you get to camp, where do you hunt, the far reaches of the property? After all no big buck would live close to camp where he might be able to keep an eye on the hunters.

There are other overlooked bucks scattered throughout much of the West, not just those mentioned here. Western whitetails are expanding their range moving into new areas where previously they have not existed, at least not in anyone's memory or history books. Quite often these small pockets of deer are populated by out-size bucks that had the opportunity to mature in the presence of extremely good nutrition. Early farmers learned crops grow and produce great yields on previously unplowed ground.

The same holds true for expanding whitetails.

Then too there are other overlooked bucks in the West, particularly the Coues and Carmen Mountains whitetails found in the Southwest. These are small-bodied and relatively small-antlered bucks that just might be the most challenging to hunt of all the whitetails.

CLOSE TO HOME WHITETAILS

On a drive back from his office in Oklahoma City, Denver McCormick started noticing several particularly large-racked bucks on the outskirts of the city limits. A couple of days later he stopped to talk to a person who was mending a stretch of fence where someone had run off the road and knocked down about 50 yards of barbed wire. With a bit of time on his hands, Denver stopped, rolled up his sleeves, and started helping the "fence mender." Yes, he owned the property and appreciated the help. No, no one hunted in the area and he was not opposed to someone hunting it, as long as they obeyed the rules. "You can hunt, but no one else can come with you. You can take one deer and I'd like to get one of the backstraps. I can't see well enough anymore to hunt, but I grew up in Texas where I learned to appreciate the taste of venison," mentioned the landowner shortly before they parted company.

Opening morning, Denver passed up eight different sizable bucks before shooting a ten-pointer that scored in the 140s with his T/C .50 caliber muzzleloader.

I suspect the same scenario has unfolded numerous times throughout the western whitetail habitat.

Cities and towns start encroaching on whitetails. They adapt to living close to people and all too often they get overlooked.

For several years I traveled to the Dallas/Fort Worth area for business purposes. During fall trips I always made a walk through a bit of country that bordered a small city lake which was not occupied by houses. Each time I did, I saw some of the best antlered whitetails I've ever seen in northern Texas, absolute monsters. Unfortunately it was within the city limits and hunting there was illegal.

Big bucks often do live within the confines of city limits. Several Boone and Crockett whitetails have been unfortunately poached within the city limits of San Antonio, Texas. I am sure the same thing has repeated itself throughout numerous states, both east and west.

As in the case with Denver, he was able to find property adjoining the city limits. With a bit of homework and asking several questions I suspect anyone could do the same.

Throughout the West more and more development or housing areas are being established near major metropolitan areas. Usually for starters, hunting is declared illegal because everyone in the development area is in love with deer. But then in time when the homeowners have had to replace expensive shrubbery numerous times or they had run into a deer with their automobiles, suddenly the deer aren't quite as "cute and cuddly" as previously imagined. During the interim bucks have grown up eating fertilized shrubs and have grown good-size antlers. Find hunting access in these areas and you stand an excellent chance to taking a good deer.

HUNTING WHERE OTHERS DON'T

One year as a biologist I manned a deer check station in South Texas. Every deer taken that year had to be "checked in," weighed, aged, and antlers measured. It was interesting duty listening to the tales told by successful hunters and where and how they took their bucks and does.

On one day, at about midafternoon, I saw a small car with one of the best deer that I had seen that year tied across the roof. The car was driven by an attractive young lady who was in near tears. When I inquired about the deer and also if there was something the matter, she unfolded her tale of woe and success.

According to her, for the past four years she had been trying to get her husband to take her to deer camp with him, knowing he dearly loved deer hunting and spent considerable time doing so each fall on a deer lease near Laredo. Finally he consented and the night before they had driven down from Houston, arriving in camp about two o'clock in the morning. About 4 a.m. her husband woke up and instructed her to dress for the morning's hunt. When dressed, they got into a pickup and drove to a lone gnarly mesquite tree in the middle of about a hundred-acre grass patch.

She did as was instructed and dutifully crawled into the tree, avoiding all but a few of the sharp thorns. Once in the mesquite, her husband handed her a rifle and before departing instructed her to stay there until he came to pick her up at noon.

With that, she watched him drive back to camp about a half mile away, walk inside the cabin, and turn off the lights. Two hours later the light came on, he reappeared and drove off, along with several other men in camp, to where they planned on hunting that morning.

Nearly an hour later it got just light enough to see and she noticed a huge rack just barely poking out of the knee-high grass about a hundred yards away. Raising the rifle she peered through the scope and just about the same time, the buck stood up to stretch. Calmly, from a solid rest against a limb, she placed the cross hairs about a third of the way down his shoulder and pulled the trigger. Down went the buck.

She continued sitting in the tree, but about nine o'clock noticed pickups starting to reappear at camp. She could easily see camp and knew she could walk there in about 15 or 20 minutes, easily. But before heading to camp she stopped to admire her buck. It was big and wide and she thought it was probably bigger than any her husband had dragged home since they had been married. While admiring the buck she happened to get a bit of blood on her slacks, dismissed it and headed to camp.

By the time she got there most of the hunters were back at camp. She listened to their stories of not seeing anything, then told them of her morning's hunt. But no one wanted to believe her until she remembered the bit of blood she had gotten on her pants. That convinced them.

Thus, the entire bunch of hunters loaded into a

pickup and headed to the broad open field. As they neared the lone mesquite they could see the curvature of a massive, many-tined beam sticking up way above the tall grass.

The hunters loudly started fussing and loudly proclaimed it was totally unfair that THIS WOMAN had come to camp and taken a big buck. Their poignant remarks were hurtful, and also directed at her husband. "How dare he bring this woman to camp and put her where she might even see deer! After all wasn't the purpose of bringing her to camp to teach her a lesson, so she'd never again want to come to deer camp!"

The husband's defense to the others in camp was, "I put her in the only area where we've never before seen a deer and where no one ever hunts."

Interesting lesson learned! I saw that same lady the following summer at a white-tailed deer exposition and walked over to talk to her and admire the mount of the monstrous buck she had taken. When I inquired as to how she was doing, she was quick to reply, "I divorced that *&*%$# husband of mine and with the money I got from the settlement started hunting on my own. Got a white-tail trip planned to Alberta this fall and also several on some really good ranches in South Texas."

A true tale told to illustrate that sometimes the best place to hunt is where others fail to go.

FAVORED OVERLOOKED PLACES

Some of my favorite hunting places are right inside the gate

Travel on horseback to reach good deer hunting areas in the high desert country of the West. Such remote and inaccessible back country offers some of the best "overlooked" buck hunting in the United States.

leading to camp, within the near proximity of camp, hunting anywhere during midday when other hunters are in camp, and hunting fairly close to major highways where others in camp don't want to hunt because of traffic noises. All these have proved ideal hunting places for not only me but some of the hunters I have guided over the years.

Why are these great places? As

already stated, bucks have learned that no one generally hunts these places or during the middle of the day. Sometimes too I think we think we know too much about whitetail behavior. Quite frankly, we think ourselves right out of hunting some of the better places.

How often have you heard tales of huge, monstrous bucks taken by first-time or rookie hunters? How did they happen to be so lucky? Well maybe they didn't know you're not suppose to hunt close to camp or houses where you can hear people talk and dogs bark. Maybe they didn't know you don't necessarily hunt relatively open field or be in the field when others know deer are not going to move.

In another chapter we discussed scouting. I think sometimes too we can scout ourselves right out of a big buck. Normally when you get a little close to a big, mature buck with your scouting, he will change his habits and throw you a curve such as moving to another nearby area where there is less human "intervention." Remember while you're trying to pattern him, he's also patterning you. And quite frankly he's better at it than we are.

BUCKS CLOSE TO CAMP

If I were a big, mature buck trying to avoid hunters I would start hanging out close to their camp. Why? Because as already mentioned, most hunters seldom if ever hunt close to camp. They normally want to go to the thickest and remotest part of the hunting territory.

Wayne Fears and I have often discussed different bucks we had known that hung out close to camp during hunting season. I know of one buck that was over 30 inches wide, with long, massive beams and tall tines that every year about the first of November, just before the season opened, showed up at an elderly Mexican couple's backyard only a short distance from a fancy hunting lodge they took care of. Every afternoon the buck ate "nubbins" of corn with the horses they kept in a small pasture adjoining their home.

Every day the hunters drove past the horse lot where the deer lived and stayed from November through January, headed to the far corners of the property in search of that particular buck. They never saw him!

That buck was one I had seen each October during the annual helicopter game survey of the property. I watched him grow from a youngster to a six- or seven-year-old monstrous buck. Each year I saw him in October several miles from where he spent the hunting season. He indeed was an interesting deer. He, I suspect, finally died of oldage, or possibly was dragged down by coyotes or ambushed by the cougar that frequented the property. I also suspect throughout the western whitetail range there are many that act and react to hunting pressure the same way he did.

A hunt in locations ignored by hunters, or in places where "conventional wisdom" says there cannot be big bucks, can produce trophy bucks like this.

Some big whitetail bucks may choose to remain close to human habitation such as farm and horse lots, outbuildings, or even hunters' camps.

If you are not hunting close to camp, consider doing so. On the worst side of what might happen, you may not see many deer, but on the other side of what might happen, you just might shoot "the house buck," one of antler dimensions everyone in camp has been looking for.

HIGHWAY AND GATE BUCKS

You may recall my telling you about the biggest typical whitetail I ever saw, one which was chasing a doe near one of the busiest highways in all of Alberta. That has not been the only big buck I've seen close to a major roadway, where the sound of traffic was so loud that it would have been distracting to most people. And not only were the bucks Denver McCormick found in near Oklahoma City close to the city limits, they lived right between two major highways. Another monstrous buck I once saw, according to the South Dakota rancher who told me about it, lived by a major Interstate and often bedded in the tall grass between the highway and the barbed wire fence next to the roadway. According to the rancher, to get to the other side of the busy road, the buck walked a short distance to an overpass, in this instance an underpass built so cattle could cross under it to

get from one side of the road to the next.

Alas, the South Dakota buck was hunted hard, but never taken. He ultimately met his fate when he was run over by an 18-wheeler, one November night after dark when he followed a young doe across the Interstate. I saw the antlers, and even with several broken tines the buck still scored 170 B&C points.

One year I watched an absolutely monstrous, nontypical Wyoming whitetail leave the area we were hunting. He ran through a big culvert under an Interstate to get the other side of the road to a unit where the hunting season had already closed. The way he acted it was not the first time he had done so.

Don't overlook hunting close to roads, but also be certain to obey the law. Some state and local regulations require being a specified distance from any roadway before you can begin hunting.

Gate bucks are also quite often overlooked. I recall a big buck that nearly everyone who hunted the property saw when they stopped to open and close the gate leading into the hunting areas. The buck generally would run across the road less than a hundred yards into the property. Everyone who saw the buck, and that included all the hunters on the ranch, talked almost in reverence about him. There campfire comments ranged from, "He's as big as any buck I've seen on the property!" to "I'd give near anything to shoot a buck like him." to "Boy, what a buck! If I ever took one that good, I'd mount him life-sized!"

Interestingly, those same hunters, who made those comments, never even attempted to hunt that buck. Why? I am totally uncertain. At the time, I was working with the property as the wildlife biologist in charge of the management plan and program. As with practically all the management programs and properties I was involved in during those years, I never hunted bucks on those properties other than obviously inferior-antlered bucks or does. I strongly believed then as now the biologist in charge of a management program should not take a big deer from the property he or she manages. Big deer should be taken by those paying for the hunting rights on that property and who pay for the implementation of the management plan. I will, however, admit that was one time I wish I had negotiated hunting rights as part of my management fees, especially since no one hunted that particular buck.

Had I hunted him I would have found a spot to set up in ambush on the road leading from the front gate and waited. I am convinced if any of the hunters on the property had done so they could have taken him. It may have required quite a bit of sitting and waiting, but he would have been worth it.

Don't do like they did and fail to hunt the buck of a lifetime simply because he was close to the road and the front gate.

PROSPECTING FOR BUCKS

Whitetails are expanding their range, especially throughout the West. Finding new pockets of bucks is not easy, but it can be done. Spend time if you can visiting with farmers and ranchers. The local feed store and rural coffee shop on the western fringes are great places to pick up tidbits about possible pockets of potentially new herds.

Prospecting takes time, but the effort and results could certainly be worth your investment!

THE TOUGHEST WESTERN WHITETAIL HUNTS

Some of the most overlooked and possibly the most challenging whitetail hunts in North America are also for two of the smaller subspecies of whitetails, the Coues, or Arizona whitetail, and the Carmen Mountains, or fantail whitetail. Both subspecies make their homes in some of the most beautiful high desert country in the world. Although both deer are reasonably numerous in their respective areas, nowhere are there tremendous numbers or concentrations of them.

Many who have hunted the "gray ghosts of the desert" consider them a poor man's desert bighorn sheep because they are no less challenging. I agree and have hunted Coues whitetail several times in the southwestern mountains of New Mexico and also in the Sierra de Madres in Sonora, Mexico. Their range essentially extends from the southwestern portion of New Mexico, down into Chihuahua and Sonora and then back north into southern Arizona.

Coues — correctly pronounced "cows" — are named after an army surgeon and are most often called "cooooes" deer, even by many of the locals. As is typical with many desert animals, they are relatively small of body but possess extremely good eyesight. Hunting them generally requires many hours of glassing and stalking to get within a reasonable shooting distance.

Interestingly when Coues whitetails are spooked they raise their tales but hold them nearly horizontal to their back, in a most curious fashion when compared to "regular" whitetails.

Their antlers are considerably smaller by comparison to those of the more northern whitetails. And their ears appear to be bigger when compared to their bodies than those found on other subspecies. Their coat of gray blends in perfectly with the gray background of their habitat and surroundings, making them extremely tough to spot.

I've hunted whitetails throughout North America and in my opinion Coues are the most challenging of all their tribe. I feel the same way about the "fantail" whitetail. Arguably they are the smallest of the whitetail subspecies and most certainly the smallest of any of the species which can be hunted. The Florida Keys deer may be smaller, but based on having seen both, my nod for the smallest goes to the Carmen Mountains whitetail.

In far western Texas in the mountains of the Big Bend, where the Carmens are found above the 4,500- foot mark, they are referred to as "fantails" and if you see one of these little deers fan his tail you'll understand why. In fact their tail is about the same length as you might find on a whitetail from Kansas or even in Michigan but, considering that mature bucks field-dress to anywhere from 50 to possibly as much as 70 pounds, with such a small body the tail indeed looks like a huge fan.

Carmen antlers are not very large by comparison to other whitetails, and like their cousin the Coues, they tend to have a massive appearance. Eight-point racks seem to be the rule, but occasionally one can be found with 10 or more points.

I've hunted the fantail both on the Texas side of the Rio Grande and also in the higher mountains of the northern part of Coahuila, Mexico. And I dearly love hunting these little deer not only because of their wariness and unique size, but also because of the fabulously beautiful terrain they live in. If you're looking for a challenging whitetail hunt for bucks that produce racks that most more northern whitetail hunters would not even take a second look at, the Coues and fantail are for you. I warn you, however, that if you do decide to make the first hunt for them, you'll want to pursue them again and again.

The Future of White-Tailed Deer Hunting

Emphasis on quality deer management may result in a greater number of extraordinary bucks like this massive 246 B&C nontypical whitetail taken in Ohio.

East

White-tailed deer hunting has never been better than it is now. We are told that there are more deer in North America now than there were when the Europeans arrived here several centuries ago. Not only are there more white-tailed deer, they have expanded their range throughout much of the continent. All of this did not just happen, far from it. White-tailed deer history in North America is a story of an animal that supplied food and necessities to Native Americans, explorers, and settlers. Then the newcomers to this land exploited the animal for its hide, its meat, and to a lessor extent its antlers. Unregulated hunting, parasites, development of land, and the lack of game law enforcement brought the deer to the brink of extinction by the late 1800s and early 1900s.

In the early 1900s those interested in wildlife, most of whom were hunters, determined that if something were not done, the white-tailed deer would soon be an animal to be seen only in books. Hunting regulations were proclaimed, game law enforcement was established, parasites such as screwworms were eradicated, stocking programs were started, refuges were set up, and hunters taxed themselves to pay for wildlife management programs. The results are a booming deer population. It is a success story about hunters coming to the aid of an animal.

Now as we enter the 21st century there are events happening that may turn this success story into a tragedy. The increasing white-tailed deer population is now clashing with mankind in ways never thought possible 75 years ago. Vehicle-deer collisions are costing lives and millions of dollars each year. Deer have become an urban pest, being called "hoofed rats" in some areas. In large numbers, they do economic damage to agricultural crops, suburban ornamental plants, and forest regeneration, as well as to their own habitat.

At the same time, the number of hunters have decreased dramatically. Antihunting sentiments are growing. Land available for wildlife and hunting is shrinking drastically and the human population continues to expand. It seems that there is a mismatch between the human dimension and the success story of the white-tailed deer.

While these facts paint a bleak picture there are many factors at work, some positive and some negative, that may give some hint to the future of this beloved creature. First lets look at some of the negative responses to the dilemma.

Nature has always dealt with overpopulation in a harsh way. Poor nutrition brought on from "too many mouths at the dinner plate" leads to large die-offs. This is usually in the form of weather extremes, disease, or parasites that attack the weakened body. Take hunting out of the picture and this would soon become a reality. Already we are dealing with a disease in eastern white-tailed deer that we know little about. Chronic Wasting Disease (CWD) has moved from the western part of North America into eastern white-tailed deer populations. Is this just the first of many natural catastrophes to befall our whitetail herds? The jury is still out on this one.

Next, we have animal rights groups wanting to spend millions of dollars on programs to sterilize deer and to trap and move deer to under-populated areas. These programs are dreamed up without the benefit of wildlife professionals being involved, and the programs show it. They would cost a fortune in dollars and manpower to attempt on a significant scale and would kill many hundreds of deer in the process. It's an uninformed layman's small attempt to solve a much larger problem.

To look at some of the positive ways our rapidly increasing deer population can be dealt with, one must first understand some basics of the natural order of wildlife. Before man got involved, there was a natural order of keeping wildlife populations within the carrying capacity of the land. It was a predator-prey relationship. Predators such as wolves and cougars fed on deer. There were lots of predators and they survived by keeping the deer populations in check. It was good for all.

When the settlers started moving into the East the predators were the first to be exterminated. They were seen as a threat to mankind and to the deer upon which man depended for food and skins. Due to this, there are few predators in the East today save one, the hunter.

To get the deer populations back to the carrying capacity of the land, the public is going to have to accept the natural order of wildlife and reestablish the predator-prey relationship. In order to do this, the role of the hunter in wildlife management is going to have to be accepted by the silent majority of citizens, those who are not hunters or antihunters. In my opinion, the antihunter will not change his negative viewpoint, so forget this minority. The education of the

Steve McKelvain dropped this B&C 148-point buck in Texas with a single-shot breechloader. Deer populations are on the rise throughout much of the United States.

non-hunter should be one of our highest priorities.

One organization that is doing a good job of this now is the Quality Deer Management Association (QDMA). Through their educational programs, they are advocating the keeping of deer populations within the carrying capacity of the land through a predator-prey relationship, sport hunting. They promote the sport harvesting of antlerless deer, and mature bucks, in prescribed numbers based on the carrying capacity of the land upon which they exist. QDMA promotes the hunter getting involved with the habitat management and population management so that he can see the importance of keeping the deer population within a healthy carrying capacity of the land. This is a growing philosophy and leads to the solution of controlling the increasing population of white-tailed deer.

Urban hunting, once unheard of, is now gaining popularity, as homeowners want relief from deer damage to shrubs and lawns. A growing number of eastern metropolitan areas are using bowhunters to

Hunting is an indispensable tool for wildlife management. Culled and managed deer herds can produce bucks like this magnificent buck.

help control their deer populations. I think we will see much more interest in urban hunting in the future, as the predator-prey message finally sinks in.

Rural landowners who want their deer populations reduced are now realizing that they cannot do it alone and this is once again opening up new hunting grounds to the responsible hunter. Since many farmers can garner much needed additional income from leasing or charging daily fees for deer hunting, this is an incentive

to open more lands for hunting.

To help the rural landowner cope with the growing deer population, many states now have a "deer management assistance program" in which the number of deer that needs to be taken from a tract of land annually to keep the population within the land's carrying capacity is determined by a deer biologist. Once that number is set, the landowner is given harvest tags that he may use to take deer during the season. These programs are doing a good job of

keeping the deer population in check, while improving the quality of deer found on the property.

As the human population continues to grow in the East, hunting acreage will shrink in size. The future will see more areas limited to hunting with bows, shotguns, and muzzleloaders due to safety concerns. Short-range hunting techniques will become more popular. This is not to say there won't be any large acreage to hunt, but there will not be as much as we have seen in the past.

I have spent almost four decades being professionally involved with both deer management and deer hunting and I have seen many changes during those years. To predict the future now is more difficult than ever. There are many positive energies at work to educate the public about the role the hunter plays in preserving a healthy deer population. We can only hope they work. I think they will, due, in part, to the problems deer are causing for the nonhunting public. I think common sense will once again kick in and the hunter will be seen in a positive way, as being a tool for wildlife management. If this happens, we will see more people deer hunting, more places to hunt, and more support for deer management programs that include hunting.

It is up to you and me to get involved in the educational efforts and show that ethical, responsible deer hunters are concerned for the sound management of the natural resource. We do have a major input into whether the future of deer hunting is positive or negative.

West

When was "The Golden Age of America's Deer?" I suspect many hunters think or thought they had lived it. That's probably been the case since the first European settlers took their first whitetails and the many hunters that have followed. I feel the same way. And maybe that truly is the case. The past 50 years, the last half of the 1900s, have seen many changes in whitetail deer populations, management practices, and public attitudes both positive and negative toward deer and deer hunting.

I remember a time in Texas during the 1950s when deer were not very plentiful. I also remember Texas a few years later experiencing severe die-offs due to starvation in what was then the most populace white-tailed deer area in the world, the Edward Plateau or Texas Hill Country. Still a few years later starting in the early and middle 1970s biologists, landowners, and hunters became interested in quality deer and quality management came into being. Soon Texas and much of the rest of North America became white-tailed deer quality conscious. Organizations, such as the Texas Trophy Hunters Association, were established to promote quality whitetails and hunting. The Stump Sitter Group in Wisconsin formed and eventually led to the formation of the *Deer & Deer Hunting* magazine. Outdoor shows such as the Dixie Deer Classic and the Texas Trophy Hunters Association's Hunter Extravaganzas led the way to a proliferation of state classics where successful hunters exhibited the best deer taken each year.

The 1980s brought great bucks and increased hunting opportunities as a result of hunter and landowner interest in deer and habitat. The "Cult of the Whitetail," unofficial though it was, seemed to form and swept the nation. Publications such as *North American Whitetail* and others started appearing on newsstands. Books, such as *Big Rack*, featuring the best whitetails taken in the past in Texas were published and soon created sufficient interest to the point that every other state and province in North America seemed to think they too needed a book of the best deer taken to prove their worth in "whitetaildom."

During this same time a huge industry was beginning to be built around the deer hunter, especially in terms of camouflage patterns and clothing as well as for scents and and lures. Hunters started traveling throughout North America in search of whitetails. Somewhere along the way landowners started charging hunters to enter their property for the purpose of hunting whitetails, not everywhere but throughout much of the whitetail's range. Hunting ranches specializing in big whitetails were established, some big and some not so big but all trying to produce the biggest possible antlered whitetail buck. Guided hunts for big whitetails started becoming popular in the mid- to late 1980s and well into the 1990s. Some guided whitetail hunting operations set their prices comparable to those previously only demanded for big horn sheep hunts and African safaris.

During a pretty good stretch of the latter part of the 1900s any outdoor publication with a big whitetail on the cover far outsold those with any other animal on the cover.

Those were particularly good and interesting times for whitetails and whitetail hunters. I am so very thankful that I came along as a wildlife biologist and hunter during those years. Whitetails provided for me not only a vocation but an avocation as well.

With the turn of the century and into the early beginning of the 2000s what lies in store for friend whitetail?

I suspect the times ahead will prove to be "interesting!"

Throughout North America, interest in whitetails is extremely high, but perhaps that interest lies in a slightly different vein than it has for the past 30 or so years.

Those who keep records of such things tell us we are at an all-time high when it comes to whitetail populations. These population highs have been brought about by favorable habitat conditions, the result of mild winters and changing weather patterns, changes in land practices conducive to whitetailed deer production, and overall interest in whitetails by hunters, wildlife watchers, and even landowners.

During the late 1900s, due to increased deer populations in several states, deer kills by automobiles equaled or exceeded hunter-bagged deer. These accidents have not only taken the lives of deer, occasionally they have also claimed the lives of people. Deer-automobile accidents have cost insurance companies and the public millions upon millions of dollars. With increases in housing and suburban development around major metropolitan

areas and even in the country into deer habitat, deer previously perceived as "brown-eyed beauties" are now being considered "brown-eyed beasties" because of deer-vehicle collisions and eating valuable landscaped shrubbery.

Attitudes are changing against deer, but also to somewhat of an extent against hunters as well. When I was growing up, the community and the media and especially television and movies showed the hunter as a hero. Many of the movie stars at the time hunted and publicly supported hunting. Back then you could tell the good guys and the bad guys by the color of their hats. White stood for good, black for bad. These days the bad guy may wear black or white hats, or no hat at all. Chances are pretty good, however, if someone is a villain, they'll portray him as a hunter.

Hunters in Hollywood are no longer vogue, but that can change practically overnight.

Statisticians tell us hunter numbers are decreasing and that the average age of hunters gets older each year. Recruitment of young hunters is down, or so they say. Part of this, if it is indeed true, is likely because finding places to hunt deer is a bit more difficult than it was many years ago and hunting has become expensive in most areas, especially if you hope to pursue big-antlered bucks. The other side of this, there is little time for parents and their children to go deer hunting, because these days youngsters are involved in organized games every weekend; baseball, soccer, basketball, football and the list of games played with balls goes on and on. Personally I don't consider these "sports." To me anything played with a ball is a "game." The only two true sports are hunting and fishing!

Whenever animal populations reach all-time highs, nature always has a way of dealing with overpopulation. Its way is one of starvation, habitat degradation brought about by too many mouths to feed, and disease and pestilence. I saw deer die by the hundreds back in the early 1970s in the Texas Hill Country. Not a pretty sight, I can assure you.

Diseases such as EHD (Epizootic Hemorrhagic Disease or Bluetongue) and other viral diseases can have a devastating effect on local deer herds and lower their overall densities, especially in areas where they have previously not come in contact with the disease.

Talk of "new" diseases such as Chronic Wasting Disease (CWD) started appearing in newspaper headlines and on television news networks in the early 2000s. While little is known about this disease, the immediate responses by game department personnel where diseased animals were found and diagnosed were no less hysterical had the news "guessers" seeking sensational headlines and stories.

Those with cooler heads and years of practical in-the-field experience with whitetail populations strongly believe that the effects of CWD if left to its own devices will not destroy deer herds as the sensationalists predict. They argue that the disease has been around for a long time but we have only now found ways to diagnose deer deaths caused by it. How will CWD play in the future? Time will tell.

The best defense to any disease problems is to maintain a healthy deer herd not stressed by nutritional problems.

Large predators such as coyotes, bobcats, cougars, wolves, and bears could be of assistance in maintaining deer populations at below what the vegetation and range can support on a sustained basis. These are "natural predators," but certainly none is a more "natural" predator than man. Unfortunately wolves, bears and cougars don't really fit well into today's world where over-populated deer herds are a major problem, quite often in and near suburbs!

It remains for man to play the part of predator and keep the populations within the capabili-

A proud hunter displays his prize of a hunt in Alberta, Canada, one of several bucks carried out of the field after a very successful hunt. Humans have been on the whitetail's list of predators for thousands of years.

ties of the deer herd's food supply. In time the public will understand.

Deer populations, hunter numbers and many other things are like the swing of a pendulum, swinging from one extreme to another. Both sides are at harmony only for a very short time when the pendulum is equidistant from both extremes.

While others may view the current problems as insurmountable, being an optimist, I see these as positives when it comes to deer and deer hunting, in the West as

well as in the East.

Landowners who previously have allowed no hunting are now opening some of their properties because they realize they cannot alone manage the deer as they should, and because there is an economic incentive for them to do so, not only among hunters but also bird and animal watchers. Here it should be noted that managing the habitat for increased variety and diversity in terms of plants certainly benefits whitetails and other game animals. But such efforts quite often benefit the non-game species even more!

Near cities and even within their boundaries, in an effort to start controlling whitetail populations, hunting opportunities are increasing and will continue to increase. Finally some of the public is beginning to understand predator-prey relationships and in the absence of predators which don't fit well with pets and children, man becomes a much more palatable predator.

Many state game departments have come to realize the importance and necessity of assigning public biologists to work with private individuals and groups in establishing and maintaining management programs aimed at deer populations and habitat. Texas has had a highly successful program of this nature since the early 1970s. Thankfully other states are seeing the value of such programs and the wildlife and habitat are benefiting from them.

Changing land practices, including more and more white-tailed deer habitat becoming human habitation, will call for changes in attitudes toward deer. These changes will also call for changes in white-tailed deer management. The size of average private properties will likely continue to shrink throughout much of the West. The kicker in the deal that will prevent continued human expansion into some areas is the fact that annual precipitation rates are low throughout much of the West, and in many areas there is little or virtually no potable subsurface water. Lack of water can be a curse but it could also be a blessing!

What will the future bring for the western whitetail and the whitetail hunter? I have great faith that the future will hold shining times. Even the pendulum will forever continue to swing back and forth. I believe those with a common-sense approach will lead the way.

How can we ensure that will happen? Become involved in decision-making processes regarding deer and habitat and support those who take a common-sense approach to deer management; be well-informed, responsible, and ethical hunters. Don't fall into the traps of knocking bowhunting, muzzleloader hunting, rifle, or handgun hunting. We're all hunters regardless of whether we hunt with string and stick, or barrel and bullet. Support hunting and proper management of deer. The future is in our hands, it's up to you and me.

Appendix

BOONE AND CROCKETT CLUB: WHITETAIL TROPHY SCORES

Founded in 1887 by Theodore Roosevelt, the Boone and Crockett Club is a nonprofit coalition of conservationists and sportsmen dedicated to addressing the issues that affect hunting, hunting conduct and ethics, wildlife, and wild habitat. In its 115-year history, the Boone and Crockett Club has been a key participant in the protection of Yellowstone, Glacier, and Denali National Parks; the creation of the National Forest Service, National Park Service, and National Wildlife Refuge System; and the establishment of the Federal Duck Stamp Program. The Boone and Crockett Club also supports educational programs that promote hunting as a vital and reliable game management tool. The club's Fair Chase philosophy calls for the ethical, sportsmanlike, and lawful pursuit and taking of free-range wild game animals in a manner that does not give the hunter an unfair advantage over the animal.

The Boone and Crockett Club also maintains records of native North American Big Game as an important conservation tool and offers an official measurement and scoring system for trophy big

game. Under the Boone & Crockett system, big game trophies, such as whitetail antlers, are measured and recorded and a numerical score is assigned based on the measurements. To enter a trophy, an original score chart must be sent to the club's office, along with an entry affidavit, score chart, photograph, and other documentation.

A hunter who wishes to enter his or her whitetail trophy with Boone and Crockett must complete one of these two forms for submission, signed and dated by a measurer appointed by Boone and Crockett. Separate forms are available for typical and nontypical white-tailed deer.

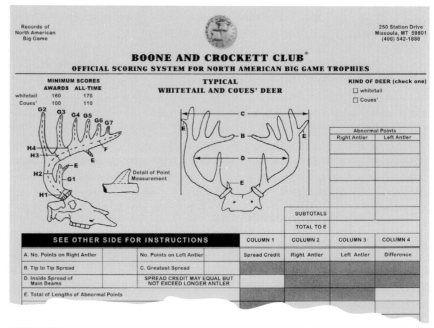

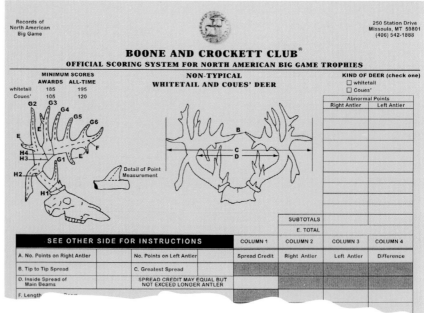

Appendix

STATE GAME AND FISH AGENCIES

Alabama
www.dcnr.state.al.us

Alaska
www.state.ak.us/local/
akpages/FISH.GAME/
ADFDHOME.HTM

Arizona
www.gf.state.az.us

Arkansas
www.agfc.state.ar.us

California
www.dfg.ca.gov

Colorado
www.dnr.state.co.us

Connecticut
www.dep.state.ct.us/
burnatr/wdhome.htm

Delaware
www.dnrec.state.de.us/
fw/huntin1.htm

Florida
www.state.fl.us/gfc

Georgia
www.dnr.state.ga.us

Hawaii
www.hawaii.gov/dlnr

Idaho
www2.state.id.us/
fishgame

Illinois
www.dnr.state.il.us

Indiana
www.state.in.us/dnr

Iowa
www.state.ia.us/
government/dnr

Kansas
www.kdwp.state.ks.us

Kentucky
www.state.ky.us/
agencies/fw/kdfwr.htm

Louisiana
www.wlf.state.la.us

Maine
www.state.me.us/ifw

Maryland
www.dnr.state.md.us

Massachusetts
www.state.ma.us/dfwele

Michigan
www.dnr.state.mi.us

Minnesota
www.dnr.state.mn.us

Mississippi
www.mdwfp.com

Missouri
www.conservation.state.
mo.us

Montana
www.fwp.mt.gov

Nebraska
www.ngpc.state.ne.us

Nevada
www.state.nv.us/cnr/
nvwildlife

New Hampshire
www.wildlife.state.nh.us

New Jersey
www.state.nj.us/dep/fgw

New Mexico
www.gmfsh.state.nm.us

New York
www.dec.state.ny.us/
website/outdoors

North Carolina
www.state.nc.us/Wildlife

North Dakota
www.state.nd.us/gnf

Ohio
www.dnr.state.oh.us

Oklahoma
www.state.ok.us/™odwc

Oregon
www.dfw.state.or.us

Pennsylvania
www.dcnr.state.pa.us

Rhode Island
www.state.ri.us/dem

South Carolina
www.water.dnr.state.
sc.us

South Dakota
www.state.sd.us/state/
executive/gfp

Tennessee
www.state.tn.us/twra

Texas
www.tpwd.state.tx.us

Utah
www.nr.state.ut.us

Vermont
www.anr.state.vt.us

Virginia
www.dgif.state.va.us

Washington
www.wa.gov/wdfw

West Virginia
www.wvwildlife.com

Wisconsin
www.dnr.state.wi.us

Wyoming
www.gf.state.wy.us

MAPPING PROGRAMS

TerraServer
www.terraserver.
microsoft.com

myTOPO.com
P. O. Box 2075
Red Lodge, MT 59068
Ph: 877-587-9004
www.mytopo.com

DeLorme
Ph: 800-569-8313
www.delorme.com

U.S. Geological Survey
P. O. Box 25286
Denver, CO 80225
Ph: 888-ask-usgs
www.usgs.gov

*Quality Deer
Management
Association*
7500-C Macon Highway
Watkinsville, GA 30677
Telephone:
1-800-209-3337
Website:
www.qdma.com

Boone & Crockett Club
The Old Milwaukee
Depot
250 Station Drive
Missoula, MT 59801
Telephone:
(406) 542-1888

Pope & Young Club
15 E. 2nd St., Box 548
Chatfield, MN 55923
Telephone:
(507) 867-4144

Index